Edward Bulwer Lytton

Kenelm Chillingly

His Adventures and Opinions

Edward Bulwer Lytton

Kenelm Chillingly
His Adventures and Opinions

ISBN/EAN: 9783742868695

Manufactured in Europe, USA, Canada, Australia, Japa

Cover: Foto ©Thomas Meinert / pixelio.de

Manufactured and distributed by brebook publishing software
(www.brebook.com)

Edward Bulwer Lytton

Kenelm Chillingly

COLLECTION

OF

BRITISH AUTHORS

TAUCHNITZ EDITION.

VOL. 1310.

KENELM CHILLINGLY

BY EDWARD BULWER, LORD LYTTON.

IN FOUR VOLUMES.

VOL. III.

KENELM CHILLINGLY

HIS

ADVENTURES AND OPINIONS

BY

EDWARD BULWER, LORD LYTTON.

COPYRIGHT EDITION.

IN FOUR VOLUMES.

VOL. III.

LEIPZIG

BERNHARD TAUCHNITZ

1873.

KENELM CHILLINGLY.

BOOK IV. *(Continued.)*

CHAPTER VI.

CHILLINGLY GORDON did not fail to confirm his acquaintance with Kenelm. He very often looked in upon him of a morning, sometimes joined him in his afternoon rides, introduced him to men of his own set who were mostly busy members of Parliament, rising barristers, or political journalists, but not without a proportion of brilliant idlers—club men, sporting men, men of fashion, rank, and fortune. He did so with a purpose, for these persons spoke well of him—spoke well not only of his talents, but of his honourable character. His general nickname amongst them was "HONEST GORDON." Kenelm at first thought this *sobriquet* must be ironical; not a bit of it. It was given to him on account of the candour and boldness with which he expressed opinions embodying that sort of cynicism which is vulgarly called "the absence of humbug." The man was certainly no hypocrite; he affected no beliefs which he did not entertain. And he had very few beliefs in anything, except the first half of the adage "Every man for himself,—and God for us all."

But whatever Chillingly Gordon's theoretical disbeliefs in things which make the current creed of the virtuous, there was nothing in his conduct which evinced predilection for vices: he was strictly upright in all his dealings, and in delicate matters of honour was a favourite umpire amongst his coevals. Though so frankly ambitious, no one could accuse him of attempting to climb on the shoulders of patrons. There was nothing servile in his nature, and though he was perfectly prepared to bribe electors if necessary, no money could have bought himself. His one master-passion was the desire of power. He sneered at patriotism as a worn-out prejudice, at philanthropy as a sentimental catch-word. He did not want to serve his country, but to rule it. He did not want to raise mankind, but to rise himself. He was therefore unscrupulous, unprincipled, as hungerers after power for itself too often are; yet still if he got power he would probably use it well, from the clearness and strength of his mental perceptions. The impression he made on Kenelm may be seen in the following letter.

TO SIR PETER CHILLINGLY, BART., ETC.

"MY DEAR FATHER,—You and my dear mother will be pleased to hear that London continues very polite to me: that 'arida nutrix leonum' enrols me among the pet class of lions which ladies of fashion admit into the society of their lap-dogs. It is somewhere about six years since I was allowed to gaze on this peep-show through the loopholes of Mr. Welby's retreat. It appears to me, perhaps erroneously, that even within that short space of time the tone of 'society' is perceptibly changed. That the change is for the better is an assertion I leave to those who belong to the *progressista* party.

"I don't think nearly so many young ladies six years ago painted their eyelids and dyed their hair: a few of them there might be, imitators of the slang invented by schoolboys and circulated through the medium of small novelists; they might use such expressions as 'stunning,' 'cheek,' 'awfully jolly,' &c. But now I find a great many who have advanced to a slang beyond that of verbal expressions,—a slang of mind, a slang of sentiment, a slang in which very little seems left of the woman, and nothing at all of the lady.

"Newspaper essayists assert that the young men of the day are to blame for this; that the young men like it, and the fair husband-anglers dress their flies in the colours most likely to attract a nibble. Whether this excuse be the true one I cannot pretend to judge. But it strikes me that the men about my own age who affect to be fast are a more languid race than the men from ten to twenty years older, whom they regard as *slow*. The habit of dram-drinking in the morning is a very new idea, an idea greatly in fashion at the moment. Adonis calls for a 'pickme-up' before he has strength enough to answer a billet-doux from Venus. Adonis has not the strength to get nobly drunk, but his delicate constitution requires stimulants, and he is always tippling.

"The men of high birth or renown for social success, belonging, my dear father, to your time, are still distinguished by an air of good-breeding, by a style of conversation more or less polished and not without evidences of literary culture, from men of the same rank in my generation, who appear to pride themselves on respecting nobody and knowing nothing, not even grammar. Still we are assured that the world goes on steadily improving. *That* new idea is in full vigour.

"Society in the concrete has become wonderfully conceited as to its own progressive excellences, and the individuals who form the concrete entertain the same complacent opinion of themselves. There are, of course, even in my brief and imperfect experience, many exceptions to what appear to me the prevalent characteristics of the rising generation in 'society.' Of these exceptions I must content myself with naming the most remarkable. *Place aux dames*, the first I name is Cecilia Travers. She and her father are now in town, and I meet them frequently. I can conceive no civilised era in the world which a woman like Cecilia Travers would not grace and adorn, because she is essentially the type of woman as man likes to imagine woman—viz., on the fairest side of the womanly character. And I say 'woman' rather than girl, because among ,Girls of the Period' Cecilia Travers cannot be classed. You might call her damsel, virgin, maiden, but you could no more call her girl than you could call a well-born French demoiselle '*fille*.' She is handsome enough to please the eye of any man, however fastidious, but not that kind of beauty which dazzles all men too much to fascinate one man; for—speaking, thank heaven, from mere theory—I apprehend that the love for woman has in it a strong sense of property; that one requires to individualise one's possession as being wholly one's own, and not a possession which all the public are invited to admire. I can readily understand how a rich man, who has what is called a show place, in which the splendid rooms and the stately gardens are open to all inspectors, so that he has no privacy in his own demesnes, runs away to a pretty cottage which he has all to himself, and of which he can say, '*This* is Home—*this* is all mine.'

"But there are some kinds of beauty which are eminently show places—which the public think they have as much a right to admire as the owner has; and the show place itself would be dull, and perhaps fall out of repair, if the public could be excluded from the sight of it.

"The beauty of Cecilia Travers is not that of a show place. There is a feeling of safety in her. If Desdemona had been like her, Othello would not have been jealous. But then Cecilia would not have deceived her father—nor I think have told a blackamoor that she wished 'Heaven had made her such a man.' Her mind harmonises with her person—it is a companionable mind. Her talents are not showy, but, take them altogether, they form a pleasant whole: she has good sense enough in the practical affairs of life, and enough of that ineffable womanly gift called tact to counteract the effects of whimsical natures like mine, and yet enough sense of the humouristic views of life not to take too literally all that a whimsical man like myself may say. As to temper, one never knows what a woman's temper is—till one puts her out of it. But I imagine hers, in its normal state, to be serene, and disposed to be cheerful. Now, my dear father, if you were not one of the cleverest of men you would infer from this eulogistic mention of Cecilia Travers that I was in love with her. But you no doubt will detect the truth, that a man in love with a woman does not weigh her merits with so steady a hand as that which guides this steel pen. I am not in love with Cecilia Travers. I wish I were. When Lady Glenalvon, who remains wonderfully kind to me, says, day after day, 'Cecilia Travers would make you a perfect wife,' I have no answer to give, but I don't feel the least inclined to ask Cecilia Travers if she would waste her perfection on one who so coldly concedes it.

"I find that she persisted in rejecting the man whom her father wished her to marry, and that he has consoled himself by marrying somebody else. No doubt other suitors as worthy will soon present themselves.

"Oh, dearest of all my friends—sole friend whom I regard as a confidant—shall I ever be in love? and if not, why not? Sometimes I feel as if, with love as with ambition, it is because I have some impossible ideal in each, that I must always remain indifferent to the sort of love and the sort of ambition which are within my reach. I have an idea that if I did love, I should love as intensely as Romeo, and that thought inspires me with vague forebodings of terror; and if I did find an object to arouse my ambition, I could be as earnest in its pursuit as—whom shall I name? —Cæsar or Cato? I like Cato's ambition the better of the two. But people nowadays call ambition an impracticable crotchet, if it be invested on the losing side. Cato would have saved Rome from the mob and the dictator; but Rome could not be saved, and Cato falls on his own sword. Had we a Cato now, the verdict at the coroner's inquest would be, 'suicide while in a state of unsound mind,' and the verdict would have been proved by his senseless resistance to a mob and a dictator! Talking of ambition, I come to the other exception to the youth of the day—I have named a demoiselle, I now name a damoiseau. Imagine a man of about five-and-twenty, and who is morally about fifty years older than a healthy man of sixty—imagine him with the brain of age and the flower of youth—with a heart absorbed into the brain, and giving warm blood to frigid ideas—a man who sneers at everything I call lofty, yet would do nothing that *he* thinks mean—to whom vice and virtue are as indifferent as they were to the Æsthetics of Goethe—who would never jeopardise his career as a practical reasoner by an imprudent virtue, and never sully his reputation by a degrading vice. Imagine this man with an intellect keen, strong, ready, unscrupulous, dauntless—all cleverness and no genius. Imagine this man, and then do not be astonished when I tell you he is a Chillingly.

"The Chillingly race culminates in him, and becomes Chillinglyest. In fact, it seems to me that we live in a day precisely suited to the Chillingly idiosyncrasies. During the ten centuries or more that our race has held local habitation and a name, it has been as airy nothings. Its representatives lived in hot-blooded times, and were compelled to skulk in still water with their emblematic Daces. But the times now, my dear father, are so cold-blooded that you can't be too cold-blooded to prosper. What could Chillingly Mivers have been in an age when people cared twopence-halfpenny about their religious creeds, and their political parties deemed their cause was sacred, and their leaders were heroes? Chillingly Mivers would not have found five subscribers to 'The Londoner.' But now 'The Londoner' is the favourite organ of the intellectucl public; it sneers away all the foundations of the social system, without an attempt at reconstruction;

and every new journal set up, if it keep its head above water, models itself on 'The Londoner.' Chillingly Mivers is a great man, and the most potent writer of the age, though nobody knows what he has written. Chillingly Gordon is a still more notable instance of the rise of the Chillingly worth in the modern market.

"There is a general impression in the most authoritative circles that Chillingly Gordon will have high rank in the van of the coming men. His confidence in himself is so thorough that it infects all with whom he comes into contact—myself included.

"He said to me the other day, with a *sang-froid* worthy of the iciest Chillingly, 'I mean to be Prime Minister of England—it is only a question of time.' Now, if Chillingly Gordon is to be Prime Minister, it will be because the increasing cold of our moral and social atmosphere will exactly suit the development of his talents.

"He is the man above all others to argue

down the declaimers of old-fashioned sentimentalities, love of country, care for its position among nations, zeal for its honour, pride in its renown (oh, if you could hear him philosophically and logically sneer away the word 'prestige'). Such notions are fast being classified as 'bosh.' And when that classification is complete—when England has no colonies to defend, no navy to pay for, no interest in the affairs of other nations, and has attained to the happy condition of Holland,—then Chillingly Gordon will be her Prime Minister.

"Yet while, if ever I am stung into political action, it will be by abnegation of the Chillingly attributes, and in opposition, however hopeless, to Chillingly Gordon, I feel that this man cannot be suppressed and ought to have fair play; his ambition will be infinitely more dangerous if it become soured by delay. I propose, my dear father, that you should have the honour of laying this clever kinsman under an obligation, and enabling him to enter Parliament. In our last conversation at Exmundham, you told me of the frank resentment of Gordon *père*, when my coming into the world shut him out from the Exmundham inheritance; you confided to me your intention at that time to lay by yearly a sum that might ultimately serve as a provision for Gordon *fils*, and as some compensation for the loss of his expectations when you realised your hope of an heir; you told me also how this generous intention on your part had been frustrated by a natural indignation at the elder Gordon's conduct in his harassing and costly litigation, and by the addition you had been tempted to make to the estate in a purchase which added to its acreage, but at a rate of interest which diminished your own income, and precluded the possibility of further savings. Now, chancing to meet your lawyer, Mr. Vining, the other day, I learned from him that it had been long a wish which your delicacy prevented your naming to me, that I, to whom the fee-simple descends, should join with you in cutting off the entail and re-settling the estate. He showed me what an advantage this would be to the property, because it would leave your hands free for many improvements in which I heartily go with the progress of the age, for which, as merely tenant for life, you could not raise the money except upon ruinous terms; new cottages for labourers, new buildings for tenants, the consolidation of some old mortgages and charges on the rent-roll, &c. And allow me to add that I should like to make a large increase to the jointure of my dear mother. Vining says too that there is a part of the outlying land which, as being near a town, could be sold to considerable profit if the estate were resettled.

"Let us hasten to complete the necessary deeds, and so obtain the £20,000 required for the realisation of your noble, and let me add, your just desire to do something for Chillingly Gordon. In the new deeds of settlement we could insure the power of willing the estate as we pleased, and I am strongly against devising it to Chillingly Gordon. It may be a crotchet of mine, but one which I think you share, that the owner of English soil should have a son's love for the native land, and Gordon will never have that. I think too that it will be best for his own career, and for the establishment of a frank understanding between us and himself, that he should be fairly told that he would not be benefited in the event of our deaths. Twenty thousand pounds given to him now would be a greater boon to him than ten times the sum twenty years later. With that at his command, he can enter Parliament, and have an income, added to what he now possesses, if modest, still sufficient to make him independent of a minister's patronage.

"Pray humour me, my dearest father, in the proposition I venture to submit to you.—Your affectionate son,

"KENELM."

FROM SIR PETER CHILLINGLY TO KENELM CHILLINGLY.

"MY DEAR BOY,—You are not worthy to be a Chillingly; you are decidedly warm-blooded: never was a load lifted off a man's mind with a gentler hand. Yes, I have wished to cut off the entail and re-settle the property, but as it was eminently to my advantage to do so, I shrank from asking it, though eventually it would be almost as much to your own advantage. What with the purchase I made of the Faircleuch lands —which I could only effect by money borrowed at high interest on my personal security, and paid off by yearly instalments, eating largely into income—and the old mortgages, &c., I own I have been pinched of late years. But what rejoices me the most is the power to make homes for our honest labourers more comfortable, and nearer to their work, which last is the chief point, for the old cottages in themselves are not bad; the misfortune is, when you build an extra room for the children, the silly people let it out to a lodger.

"My dear boy, I am very much touched by your wish to increase your mother's jointure—a very proper wish, independently of filial feeling, for she brought to the estate a very pretty fortune, which the Trustees consented to my investing in land; and though the land completed our ring-fence, it does not bring in two per cent, and the conditions of the entail limited the right of jointure to an amount below that which a widowed Lady Chillingly may fairly expect.

"I care more about the provision on these points than I do for the interests of old Chillingly Gordon's son. I had meant to behave very handsomely to the father, and when the return for behaving handsomely is being put into Chancery—A Worm Will Turn. Nevertheless, I agree with you that a son should not be punished for his father's faults, and if the sacrifice of £20,000 makes you and myself feel that we are better Christians and truer gentlemen, we shall buy that feeling very cheaply."

Sir Peter then proceeded, half-jestingly, half-seriously, to combat Kenelm's declaration that he was not in love with Cecilia Travers, and, urging the advantages of marriage with one whom Kenelm allowed would be a perfect wife, astutely remarked, that unless Kenelm had a son of his own, it did not seem to him quite just to the next of kin to will the property from him, upon no better plea than the want of love for his native country. "He would love his country fast enough if he had 10,000 acres in it."

Kenelm shook his head when he came to this sentence.

"Is even, then, love for one's country but cupboard love after all?" said he; and he postponed finishing the perusal of his father's letter.

CHAPTER VII.

Kenelm Chillingly did not exaggerate the social position he had acquired when he classed himself amongst the lions of the fashionable world. I dare not count the number of three-cornered notes showered upon him by the fine ladies who grow romantic upon any kind of celebrity; or the carefully-sealed envelopes, containing letters from fair anonymas, who asked if he had a heart, and would be in such a place in the Park at such an hour. What there was in Kenelm Chillingly that should make him thus favoured, especially by the fair sex, it would be difficult to say, unless it was the twofold reputation of being unlike other people, and of being unaffectedly indifferent to the gain of any reputation at all. He might, had he so pleased, have easily established a proof that the prevalent though vague belief in his talents was not altogether unjustified. For the articles he had sent from abroad to 'The Londoner,' and by which his travelling expenses were defrayed, had been stamped by that sort of originality in tone and treatment which rarely fails to excite curiosity as to the author, and meets with more general praise than perhaps it deserves.

But Mivers was true to his contract to preserve inviolable the incognito of the author, and Kenelm regarded with profound contempt the articles themselves, and the readers who praised them.

Just as misanthropy with some persons grows out of benevolence disappointed, so there are certain natures—and Kenelm Chillingly's was perhaps one of them—in which indifferentism grows out of earnestness baffled.

He had promised himself pleasure in renewing acquaintance with his old tutor, Mr. Welby —pleasure in refreshing his own taste for metaphysics and casuistry and criticism. But that accomplished professor of realism had retired from philosophy altogether, and was now enjoying a holiday for life in the business of a public office. A Minister in favour of whom, when in opposition, Mr. Welby, in a moment of whim, wrote some very able articles in a leading journal, had, on acceding to power, presented the realist with one of those few good things still left to Ministerial patronage—a place worth about £1200 a-year. His mornings thus engaged in routine work, Mr. Welby enjoyed his evenings in a convivial way.

"*Inveni portum*," he said to Kenelm; "I plunge into no troubled waters now. But come and dine with me to-morrow, *tête-à-tête*. My wife is at St. Leonard's with my youngest born for the benefit of sea-air." Kenelm accepted the invitation.

The dinner would have contented a Brillat-Savarin—it was faultless; and the claret was that rare nectar, the Lafitte of 1848.

"I never share this," said Welby, "with more than one friend at a time."

Kenelm sought to engage his host in discussion on certain new works in vogue, and which were composed according to purely realistic canons of criticism. "The more realistic these books pretend to be, the less real they are," said Kenelm. "I am half inclined to think that the whole school you so systematically sought to build up is a mistake, and that realism in art is a thing impossible."

"I daresay you are right. I took up that school in earnest because I was in a passion with pretenders to the Idealistic school, and whatever one takes up in earnest is generally a mistake, especially if one is in a passion. I was not in earnest and I was not in a passion when I wrote those articles to which I am indebted for my office." Mr. Welby here luxuriously stretched his limbs, and lifting his glass to his lips, voluptuously inhaled its *bouquet*.

"You sadden me," returned Kenelm. "It is a melancholy thing to find that one's mind was influenced in youth by a teacher who mocks at his own teachings."

Welby shrugged his shoulders. "Life consists in the alternate process of learning and unlearning; but it is often wiser to unlearn than to learn. For the rest, as I have ceased to be a critic, I care little whether I was wrong or right when I played that part. I think I am right now as a placeman. Let the world go its own way, provided the world lets you live upon it. I drain my wine to the lees, and cut down hope to the brief span of life. Reject realism in art if you please, and accept realism in conduct. For the first time in my life I am comfortable: my mind having worn out its walking-shoes, is now enjoying the luxury of slippers. Who can deny the realism of comfort?"

"Has a man a right," Kenelm said to himself, as he entered his brougham, "to employ all the brilliancy of a rare wit—all the acquisitions of as rare a scholarship—to the scaring of the young generation out of the safe old roads which youth left to itself would take—old roads skirted by romantic rivers and bowery trees—directing them into new paths on long sandy flats, and then, when they are faint and footsore, to tell them that he cares not a pin whether they have worn out their shoes in right paths or wrong paths, for that he has attained the *summum bonum* of philosophy in the comfort of easy slippers?"

Before he could answer the question he thus put to himself, his brougham stopped at the door of the Minister whom Welby had contributed to bring into power.

That night there was a crowded muster of the fashionable world at the great man's house. It happened to be a very critical moment for the Minister. The fate of his Cabinet depended on the result of a motion about to be made the following week in the House of Commons. The great man stood at the entrance of the apartments to receive his guests, and among the guests were the framers of the hostile motion and the leaders of the Opposition. His smile was not less gracious to them than to his dearest friends and staunchest supporters.

"I suppose this is realism," said Kenelm to himself; "but it is not truth, and it is not comfort." Leaning against the wall near the doorway, he contemplated with grave interest the striking countenance of his distinguished host. He detected beneath that courteous smile and that urbane manner the signs of care. The eye was absent, the cheek pinched, the brow furrowed. Kenelm turned away his looks, and glanced over the animated countenances of the idle loungers along commoner thoroughfares in life. Their eyes were not absent, their brows were not furrowed; their minds seemed quite at home in exchanging nothings. Interest many of them had in the approaching struggle, but it was much such an interest as betters of small sums may have on the Derby day—just enough to give piquancy to the race; nothing to make gain a great joy, or loss a keen anguish.

"Our host is looking ill," said Mivers, accosting Kenelm. "I detect symptoms of suppressed gout. You know my aphorism, 'nothing so gouty as ambition,' especially parliamentary ambition."

"You are not one of those friends who press on my choice of life that source of disease; allow me to thank you."

"Your thanks are misplaced. I strongly advise you to devote yourself to a political career."

"Despite the gout?"

"Despite the gout. If you could take the world as I do, my advice might be different. But your mind is overcrowded with doubts and fantasies and crotchets, and you have no choice but to give them vent in active life."

"You had something to do in making me what I am—an idler; something to answer for as to my doubts, fantasies, and crotchets. It was by your recommendation that I was placed under the tuition of Mr. Welby, and at that critical age in which the bent of the twig forms the shape of the tree."

"And I pride myself on that counsel. I repeat the reasons for which I gave it: it is an incalculable advantage for a young man to start in life thoroughly initiated into the New Ideas which will more or less influence his generation. Welby was the ablest representative of these ideas. It is a wondrous good fortune when the propagandist of the New Ideas is something more than a bookish philosopher—when he is a thorough 'man of the world,' and is what we emphatically call 'practical.' Yes, you owe me much that I secured to you such tuition, and saved you from twaddle and sentiment, the poetry of Wordsworth and the muscular Christianity of cousin John."

"What you say that you saved me from might have done me more good than all you conferred on me. I suspect that when education succeeds in placing an old head upon young shoulders, the combination is not healthful—it clogs the blood and slackens the pulse. However, I must not be ungrateful; you meant kindly. Yes, I suppose Welby is practical; he has no belief, and he has got a place. But our host, I presume, is also practical; his place is a much higher one than Welby's, and yet he surely is not without belief?"

"He was born before the new ideas came into practical force; but in proportion as they have done so, his beliefs have necessarily disappeared. I don't suppose that he believes in much now, except the two propositions: firstly, that if he accept the new ideas, he will have power and keep it, and if he does not accept them, power is out of the question; and secondly, that if the new ideas are to prevail, he is the best man to direct them safely—beliefs quite enough for a Minister. No wise Minister should have more."

"Does he not believe that the motion he is to resist next week is a bad one?"

"A bad one of course, in its consequences, for if it succeed it will upset him; a good one in itself I am sure he must think it, for he would bring it on himself if he were in opposition."

"I see that Pope's definition is still true, 'Party is the madness of the many for the gain of the few.'"

"No, it is not true. Madness is a wrong word applied to the many; the many are sane enough—they know their own objects, and they make use of the intellect of the few in order to gain their objects. In each party it is the many that control the few who nominally lead them. A man becomes Prime Minister because he seems to the many of his party the fittest person to carry out their views. If he presume to differ from these views, they put him into a moral pillory, and pelt him with their dirtiest stones and their rottenest eggs."

"Then the maxim should be reversed, and party is rather the madness of the few for the gain of the many?"

"Of the two, that is the more correct definition."

"Let me keep my senses and decline to be one of the few."

Kenelm moved away from his cousin's side, and entering one of the less crowded rooms, saw Cecilia Travers seated there in a recess with Lady Glenalvon. He joined them, and after a brief interchange of a few commonplaces, Lady Glenalvon quitted her post to accost a foreign ambassadress, and Kenelm sunk into the chair she vacated.

It was a relief to his eye to contemplate Cecilia's candid brow; to his ear to hearken to the soft voice that had no artificial tones, and uttered no cynical witticisms.

"Don't you think it strange," said Kenelm, "that we English should so mould all our habits as to make even what we call pleasure as little pleasurable as possible? We are now in the beginning of June, the fresh outburst of summer, when every day in the country is a delight to eye and ear, and we say, 'the season for hot rooms is beginning.' We alone of civilised races spend our summer in a capital, and cling to the country when the trees are leafless and the brooks frozen."

"Certainly that is a mistake; but I love the country in all seasons, even in winter."

"Provided the country house is full of London people?"

"No; that is rather a drawback. I never want companions in the country."

"True; I should have remembered that you differ from young ladies in general, and make companions of books. They are always more conversible in the country than they are in town;

or rather, we listen there to them with less distracted attention. Ha! do I not recognise yonder the fair whiskers of George Belvoir? Who is the lady leaning on his arm?"

"Don't you know?—Lady Emily Belvoir, his wife."

"Ah! I was told that he had married. The lady is handsome. She will become the family diamonds. Does she read Blue Books?"

"I will ask her if you wish."

"Nay, it is scarcely worth while. During my rambles abroad, I saw but few English newspapers. I did, however, learn that George had won his election. Has he yet spoken in Parliament?"

"Yes; he moved the answer to the address this session, and was much complimented on the excellent tone and taste of his speech. He spoke again a few weeks afterwards, I fear not so successfully."

"Coughed down?"

"Something like it."

"Do him good; he will recover the cough, and fulfil my prophecy of his success."

"Have you done with poor George for the present? If so, allow me to ask whether you have quite forgotten Will Somers and Jessie Wiles?"

"Forgotten them! no."

"But you have never asked after them?"

"I took it for granted that they were as happy as could be expected. Pray assure me that they are."

"I trust so now; but they have had trouble, and have left Graveleigh."

"Trouble! left Graveleigh! You make me uneasy. Pray explain."

"They had not been three months married and installed in the home they owed to you, when poor Will was seized with a rheumatic fever. He was confined to his bed for many weeks; and when at last he could move from it, was so weak as to be still unable to do any work. During his illness Jessie had no heart, and little leisure to attend to the shop. Of course I—that is, my dear father—gave them all necessary assistance; but——"

"I understand; they were reduced to objects of charity. Brute that I am, never to have thought of the duties I owed to the couple I had brought together. But pray go on."

"You are aware that just before you left us my father received a proposal to exchange his property at Graveleigh for some lands more desirable to him?"

"I remember. He closed with that offer."

"Yes; Captain Stavers, the new landlord of Graveleigh, seems to be a very bad man, and though he could not turn the Somerses out of the cottage so long as they paid rent—which we took care they did pay—yet out of a very wicked spite he set up a rival shop in one of his other cottages in the village, and it became impossible for these poor young people to get a livelihood at Graveleigh."

"What excuse for spite against so harmless a young couple could Captain Stavers find or invent?"

Cecilia looked down and coloured. "It was a revengeful feeling against Jessie."

"Ah! I comprehend."

"But they have now left the village, and are happily settled elsewhere. Will has recovered his health, and they are prospering—much more than they could ever have done at Graveleigh."

"In that change you were their benefactress, Miss Travers?" said Kenelm, in a more tender voice and with a softer eye than he had ever before evinced towards the heiress.

"No, it is not I whom they have to thank and bless.

"Who, then, is it? Your father?"

"No. Do not question me; I am bound not to say. They do not themselves know; they rather believe that their gratitude is due to you."

"To me! Am I to be for ever a sham in spite of myself? My dear Miss Travers, it is essential to my honour that I should undeceive this credulous pair; where can I find them?"

"I must not say; but I will ask permission of their concealed benefactor, and send you their address."

A touch was laid on Kenelm's arm, and a voice whispered—"May I ask you to present me to Miss Travers?"

"Miss Travers," said Kenelm, "I entreat you to add to the list of your acquaintances a cousin of mine—Mr. Chillingly Gordon."

While Gordon addressed to Cecilia the well-bred conventionalisms with which acquaintance in London drawing-rooms usually commences, Kenelm, obedient to a sign from Lady Glenalvon, who had just re-entered the room, quitted his seat, and joined the Marchioness.

"Is not that young man whom you left talking with Miss Travers your clever cousin Gordon?"

"The same."

"She is listening to him with great attention. How his face brightens up as he talks. He is positively handsome, thus animated."

"Yes, I could fancy him a dangerous wooer. He has wit, and liveliness, and audacity; he could be very much in love with a great fortune, and talk to the owner of it with a fervour rarely exhibited by a Chillingly. Well, it is no affair of mine."

"It ought to be."

"Alas and alas! that 'ought to be;' what depths of sorrowful meaning lie within that simple phrase! How happy would be our lives, how grand our actions, how pure our souls, if all could be with us as it ought to be!"

CHAPTER VIII.

We often form cordial intimacies in the confined society of a country-house, or a quiet watering-place, or a small Continental town, which fade away into remote acquaintanceship in the mighty vortex of London life, neither party being to blame for the estrangement. It was so with Leopold Travers and Kenelm Chillingly. Travers, as we have seen, had felt a powerful charm in the converse of the young stranger, so in contrast with the routine of the rural companionships to which his alert intellect had for many years circumscribed its range. But, on reappearing in London the season before Kenelm again met him, he had renewed old friendships with men of his own standing,—officers in the regiment of which he had once been a popular ornament, some of them still unmarried, a few of them like himself, widowed; others, who had been his rivals in fashion, and were still pleasant idlers about town; and it rarely happens in a metropolis that we have intimatė friendships with those of another generation, unless there be some common tie in the cultivation of art and letters, or the action of kindred sympathies in the party strife of politics. Therefore Travers and Kenelm had had little familiar communication with each other since they first met at the Beaumanoirs'. Now and then they found themselves at the same crowded assemblies, and interchanged nods and salutations. But their habits were different. The houses at which they were intimate were not the same; neither did they frequent the same clubs. Kenelm's chief bodily exercise was still that of long and early rambles into rural suburbs; Leopold's was that of a late ride in the Row. Of the two, Leopold was much more the man of pleasure. Once restored to metropolitan life, a temper constitutionally eager, ardent, and convivial, took kindly, as in earlier youth, to its light range of enjoyments.

Had the intercourse between the two men

been as frankly familiar as it had been at Neesdale Park, Kenelm would probably have seen much more of Cecilia at her own home; and the admiration and esteem with which she already inspired him might have ripened into much warmer feeling, had he thus been brought into clearer comprehension of the soft and womanly heart, and its tender predisposition towards himself.

He had said somewhat vaguely in his letter to Sir Peter that "sometimes he felt as if his indifference to love, as to ambition, was because he had some impossible ideal in each." Taking that conjecture to task, he could not honestly persuade himself that he had formed any ideal of woman and wife with which the reality of Cecilia Travers was at war. On the contrary, the more he thought over the characteristics of Cecilia, the more they seemed to correspond to any ideal that had floated before him in the twilight of dreamy reverie, and yet he knew that he was not in love with her, that his heart did not respond to his reason. And mournfully he resigned himself to the conviction that nowhere in this planet, from the normal pursuits of whose inhabitants he fell so estranged, was there waiting for him the smiling playmate, the earnest helpmate. As this conviction strengthened, so an increased weariness of the artificial life of the metropolis, and of all its objects and amusements, turned his thoughts with an intense yearning towards the Bohemian freedom and fresh excitements of his foot ramblings. He often thought with envy of the wandering minstrel, and wondered whether, if he again traversed the same range of country, he might encounter again that vagrant singer.

CHAPTER IX.

It is nearly a week since Kenelm had met Cecilia, and he is sitting in his rooms with Lord Thetford at that hour of three in the afternoon which is found the most difficult to dispose of by idlers about town. Amongst young men of his own age and class with whom Kenelm assorted in the fashionable world, perhaps the one whom he liked the best, and of whom he saw the most, was this young heir of the Beaumanoirs; and though Lord Thetford has nothing to do with the direct stream of my story, it is worth pausing a few minutes to sketch an outline of one of the best whom the last generation has produced for a part that, owing to accidents of birth and fortune, young men like Lord Thetford must play on that stage from which the curtain is not yet drawn up. Destined to be the head of a family that unites with princely possessions and an historical name a keen though honourable ambition for political power, Lord Thetford has been carefully educated, especially in the new ideas of his time. His father, though a man of no ordinary talents, has never taken a prominent part in public life. He desires his eldest son to do so. The Beaumanoirs have been Whigs from the time of William III. They have shared the good and the ill fortunes of a party which, whether we side with it or not, no politician who dreads extremes in the Government of a State, so pre-eminently artificial that a prevalent extreme at either end of the balance would be fatal to equilibrium, can desire to become extinct or feeble so long as a constitutional monarchy exists in England. From the reign of George I. to the death of George IV., the Beaumanoirs were in the ascendant. Visit their family portrait-gallery, and you must admire the eminence of a house which, during that interval of less than a century, contributed so many men to the service of the State or the adornment of the Court—so many Ministers, Ambassadors, Generals, Lord Chamberlains, and

Masters of the Horse. When the younger Pitt beat the great Whig Houses, the Beaumanoirs vanish into comparative obscurity; they re-emerge with the accession of William IV., and once more produce bulwarks of the State and ornaments of the Crown. The present Lord of Beaumanoir, *poco curante* in politics though he be, has at least held high offices at Court; and, as a matter of course, he is Lord-Lieutenant of his county, as well as Knight of the Garter. He is a man whom the chiefs of his party have been accustomed to consult on critical questions. He gives his opinions confidentially and modestly, and when they are rejected never takes offence. He thinks that a time is coming when the head of the Beaumanoirs should descend into the lists and fight hand-to-hand with any Hodge or Hobson in the cause of his country for the benefit of the Whigs. Too lazy or too old to do this himself, he says to his son, "You must do it: without effort of mine the thing may last my life. It needs effort of yours that the thing may last through your own."

Lord Thetford cheerfully responds to the

paternal admonition. He curbs his natural inclinations, which are neither inelegant nor unmanly; for, on the one side he is very fond of music and painting, an accomplished amateur, and deemed a sound connoisseur in both; and on the other side he has a passion for all field sports, and especially for hunting. He allows no such attractions to interfere with diligent attention to the business of the House of Commons. He serves in Committees, he takes the chair at public meetings on sanitary questions, or projects for social improvement, and acquits himself well therein. He has not yet spoken in debate, but he has been only two years in Parliament, and he takes his father's wise advice not to speak till the third. But he is not without weight among the well-born youth of the party, and has in him the stuff out of which, when it becomes seasoned, the Corinthian capitals of a Cabinet may be very effectively carved. In his own heart he is convinced that his party are going too far and too fast; but with that party he goes on light-heartedly, and would continue to do so if they went to

Erebus. But he would prefer their going the other way. For the rest, a pleasant bright-eyed young fellow, with vivid animal spirits; and, in the holiday moments of reprieve from public duty, he brings sunshine into draggling hunting-fields, and a fresh breeze into heated ball-rooms.

"My dear fellow," said Lord Thetford, as he threw aside his cigar, "I quite understand that you bore yourself—you have nothing else to do!"

"What can I do?"

"Work."

"Work!"

"Yes, you are clever enough to feel that you have a mind; and mind is a restless inmate of body—it craves occupation of some sort, and regular occupation too; it needs its daily constitutional exercise. Do you give your mind that?"

"I am sure I don't know, but my mind is always busying itself about something or other."

"In a desultory way—with no fixed object."

"True."

"Write a book, and then it will have its constitutional."

"Nay, my mind is always writing a book (though it may not publish one), always jotting down impressions, or inventing incidents, or investigating characters; and between you and me, I do not think that I do bore myself so much as I did formerly. Other people bore me more than they did."

"Because you will not create an object in common with other people: come into Parliament, side with a party, and you have that object."

"Do you mean seriously to tell me that you are not bored in the House of Commons."

"With the speakers very often, yes; but with the strife between the speakers, no. The House of Commons life has a peculiar excitement scarcely understood out of it; but you may conceive its charm when you observe that a man who has once been in the thick of it feels forlorn and shelved if he lose his seat, and even repines when the accident of birth transfers him to the serener air of the Upper House. Try that life, Chillingly."

"I might if I were an ultra-Radical, a Republican, a Communist, a Socialist, and wished to upset everything existing, for then the strife would at least be a very earnest one!"

"But could not you be equally in earnest against those revolutionary gentlemen?"

"Are you and your leaders in earnest against them? They don't appear to me so."

Thetford was silent for a minute. "Well, if you doubt the principles of my side, go with the other side. For my part, I and many of our party would be glad to see the Conservatives stronger."

"I have no doubt they would. No sensible man likes to be carried off his legs by the rush of the crowd behind him; and a crowd is less headlong when it sees a strong force arrayed against it in front. But it seems to me that, at present, Conservatism can but be what it now is—a party that may combine for resistance, and will not combine for inventive construction. We are living in an age in which the process of unsettlement is going blindly at work, as if impelled by a Nemesis as blind as itself. New ideas come beating in surf and surge against those which former reasoners had considered as fixed banks and breakwaters; and the new ideas are so mutable, so fickle, that those which were considered novel ten years ago, are deemed obsolete to-day, and the new ones of to-day will in their turn be obsolete to-morrow. And, in a sort of fatalism, you see statesmen yielding way to these successive mockeries of experiment—for they are experiments against experience—and saying to each other with a shrug of the shoulders, 'Bismillah, it must be so; the country will have it, even though it sends the country to the dogs.' I don't feel sure that the country will not go there the sooner, if you can only strengthen the Conservative element enough to set it up in office, with the certainty of knocking it down again. Alas, I am too dispassionate a looker-on to be fit for a partisan; would I were not. Address yourself to my cousin Gordon."

"Ay, Chillingly Gordon is a coming man, and has all the earnestness you find absent in party and in yourself."

"You call him earnest?"

"Thoroughly, in the pursuit of one object—the advancement of Chillingly Gordon. If he get into the House of Commons, and succeed there, I hope he will never become my leader, for if he thought Christianity in the way of his promotion, he would bring in a bill for its abolition."

"In that case would he still be your leader?"

"My dear Kenelm, you don't know what is the spirit of party, and how easily it makes excuses for any act of its leader. Of course, if Gordon brought in a bill for the abolition of Christianity, it would be on the plea that the abolition was good for the Christians, and his followers would cheer that enlightened sentiment."

"Ah," said Kenelm, with a sigh, "I own myself the dullest of blockheads; for instead of tempting me into the field of party politics, your talk leaves me in stolid amaze that you do not take to your heels, where honour can only be saved by flight."

"Pooh, my dear Chillingly, we cannot run away from the age in which we live—we must accept its conditions and make the best of them; and if the House of Commons be nothing else, it is a famous debating society and a capital club. Think over it. I must leave you now. I am going to see a picture at the Exhibition which has been most truculently criticised in 'The Londoner,' but which I am assured, on good authority, is a work of remarkable merit. I can't bear to see a man snarled and sneered down, no doubt by jealous rivals, who have their influence in journals, so I shall judge of the picture for myself. If it be really as good as I am told, I shall talk about it to everybody I meet—and in matters of art I fancy my word goes for something. Study art, my dear Kenelm. No gentleman's education is complete if he don't know a good picture from a bad one. After the Exhibition I shall just have time for a canter round the

Park before the debate of the session, which begins to-night."

With a light step the young man quitted the room, humming an air from the 'Figaro' as he descended the stairs. From the window Kenelm watched him swinging himself with careless grace into his saddle and riding briskly down the street —in form and face and bearing, a very model of young, high-born, high-bred manhood. "The Venetians," muttered Kenelm, "decapitated Marino Faliero for conspiring against his own order —the nobles. The Venetians loved their institutions, and had faith in them. Is there such love and such faith among the English?"

As he thus soliloquised he heard a shrilling sort of squeak; and a showman stationed before his window the stage on which Punch satirises the laws and moralities of the world, "kills the beadle and defies the devil."

CHAPTER X.

KENELM turned from the sight of Punch and Punch's friend the cur, as his servant, entering, said, "A person from the country, who would not give his name, asked to see him."

Thinking it might be some message from his father, Kenelm ordered the stranger to be admitted, and in another minute there entered a young man of handsome countenance and powerful frame, in whom, after a surprised stare, Kenelm recognised Tom Bowles. Difficult indeed would have been that recognition to an unobservant beholder: no trace was left of the sullen bully or the village farrier; the expression of the face was mild and intelligent—more bashful than hardy; the brute strength of the form had lost its former clumsiness, the simple dress was that of a gentleman—to use an expressive idiom, the whole man was wonderfully "toned down."

"I am afraid, sir, I am taking a liberty," said Tom, rather nervously, twiddling his hat between his fingers.

"I should be a greater friend to liberty than I am if it were always taken in the same way," said Kenelm, with a touch of his saturnine humour; but then yielding at once to the warmer impulse of his nature, he grasped his old antagonist's hand and exclaimed, "My dear Tom, you are so welcome. I am so glad to see you. Sit down, man; sit down—make yourself at home."

"I did not know you were back in England, sir, till within the last few days; for you did say that when you came back I should see or hear from you," and there was a tone of reproach in the last words.

"I am to blame, forgive me," said Kenelm remorsefully. "But how did you find me out? you did not then, I think, even know my name. That, however, it was easy enough to discover; but who gave you my address in this lodging?"

"Well, sir, it was Miss Travers; and she bade me come to you. Otherwise, as you did not send for me, it was scarcely my place to call uninvited."

"But, my dear Tom, I never dreamed that you were in London. One don't ask a man whom one supposes to be more than a hundred miles off to pay one an afternoon call. You are still with your uncle, I presume? And I need not ask if all thrives well with you—you look a prosperous man, every inch of you, from crown to toe."

"Yes," said Tom; "thank you kindly, sir, I am doing well in the way of business, and my uncle is to give me up the whole concern at Christmas."

While Tom thus spoke Kenelm had summoned his servant, and ordered up such refreshments as could be found in the larder of a bachelor in lodgings. "And what brings you to town, Tom?"

"Miss Travers wrote to me about a little business which she was good enough to manage for me, and said you wished to know about it; and so, after turning it over in my mind for a few days, I resolved to come to town: indeed," added Tom, heartily, "I did wish to see your face again."

"But you talk riddles. What business of yours could Miss Travers imagine I wished to know about?"

Tom coloured high, and looked very embarrassed. Luckily the servant here entering with the refreshment tray, allowed him time to recover himself. Kenelm helped him to a liberal slice of cold pigeon-pie, pressed wine on him, and did not renew the subject till he thought his guest's tongue was likely to be more freely set loose; then he said, laying a friendly hand on Tom's shoulder, "I have been thinking over what passed between me and Miss Travers. I wished to have the new address of Will Somers; she promised to write to his benefactor to ask permission to give it. You are that benefactor?"

"Don't say benefactor, sir. I will tell you how it came about if you will let me. You see, I sold my little place at Graveleigh to the new Squire, and when mother removed to Luscombe to be near me, she told me how poor Jessie had been annoyed by Captain Stavers, who seems to think his purchase included the young women on the property along with the standing timber; and I was half afraid that she had given some cause for his persecution, for you know she has a blink of those soft eyes of hers that might charm a wise man out of his skin, and put a fool there instead."

"But I hope she has done with those blinks since her marriage."

"Well, and I honestly think she has. It is certain she did not encourage Captain Stavers, for I went over to Graveleigh myself on the sly, and lodged concealed with one of the cottagers who owed me a kindness; and one day, as I was at watch, I saw the Captain peering over the stile which divides Holmwood from the glebe—you remember Holmwood?"

"I can't say I do."

"The footway from the village to Squire Travers' goes through the wood, which is a few hundred yards at the back of Will Somers' orchard.

Presently the Captain drew himself suddenly back from the stile, and disappeared among the trees, and then I saw Jessie coming from the orchard with a basket over her arm, and walking quick towards the wood. Then, sir, my heart sunk. I felt sure she was going to meet the Captain. However, I crept along the hedgerow, hiding myself, and got into the wood almost as soon as Jessie got there, by another way. Under the cover of the brushwood I stole on till I saw the Captain come out from the copse on the other side of the path, and plant himself just before Jessie. Then I saw at once I had wronged her. She had not expected to see him, for she hastily turned back, and began to run homeward; but he caught her up, and seized her by the arm. I could not hear what he said, but I heard her voice quite sharp with fright and anger. And then he suddenly seized her round the waist, and she screamed, and I sprang forward——"

"And thrashed the Captain?"

"No, I did not," said Tom; "I had made a vow to myself that I never would be violent again if I could help it. So I took him with one hand by the cuff of the neck, and with the other by the waistband, and just pitched him on a bramble bush—quite mildly. He soon picked himself up, for he is a dapper little chap, and became very blustering and abusive. But I kept my temper, and said civilly, 'Little gentleman, hard words break no bones; but if ever you molest Mrs. Somers again, I will carry you into her orchard, souse you into the duckpond there, and call all the villagers to see you scramble out of it again; and I will do it now if you are not off. I daresay you have heard of my name—I am Tom Bowles.' Upon that, his face, which was before very red, grew very white, and muttering something I did not hear, he walked away.

"Jessie—I mean Mrs. Somers—seemed at first as much frightened at me as she had been at the Captain; and though I offered to walk with her to Miss Travers, where she was going with a basket which the young lady had ordered, she refused, and went back home. I felt hurt, and returned to my uncle's the same evening; and it was not for months that I heard the Captain had been spiteful enough to set up an opposition shop, and that poor Will had been taken ill, and his wife was confined about the same time, and the talk was that they were in distress, and might have to be sold up.

"When I heard all this, I thought that after all it was my rough tongue that had so angered the Captain and been the cause of his spite, and so it was my duty to make it up to poor Will and his wife. I did not know how to set about mending matters, but I thought I'd go and talk to Miss Travers; and if ever there was a kind heart in a girl's breast, hers is one."

"You are right there, I guess. What did Miss Travers say?"

"Nay; I hardly know what she did say, but she set me thinking, and it struck me that Jessie —Mrs. Somers—had better move to a distance, and out of the Captain's reach, and that Will would do better in a less out-of-the-way place. And then, by good luck, I read in the newspaper that a stationery and fancy-work business, with a circulating library, was to be sold on moderate terms at Moleswich, the other side of London. So I took the train and went to the place, and thought the shop would just suit these young folks, and not be too much work for either; then I went to Miss Travers, and I had a lot of money lying by me from the sale of the old forge and premises, which I did not know what to do with; and so, to cut short a long story, I bought the business, and Will and his wife are settled at Moleswich, thriving and happy, I hope, sir."

Tom's voice quivered at the last words, and he turned aside quickly, passing his hand over his eyes.

Kenelm was greatly moved.

"And they don't know what you did for them?"

"To be sure not. I don't think Will would have let himself be beholden to me. Ah, the lad has a spirit of his own, and Jessie—Mrs. Somers—would have felt pained and humbled that I should even think of such a thing. Miss Travers managed it all. They take the money as a loan which is to be paid by instalments. They have sent Miss Travers more than one instalment already, so I know they are doing well."

"A loan from Miss Travers?"

"No; Miss Travers wanted to have a share in it, but I begged her not. It made me happy to do what I did all myself; and Miss Travers felt for me and did not press. They perhaps think it is Squire Travers (though he is not a man who would like to say it, for fear it should bring applicants on him), or some other gentleman who takes an interest in them."

"I always said you were a grand fellow, Tom. But you are grander still than I thought you."

"If there be any good in me, I owe it to you, sir. Think what a drunken, violent brute I was when I first met you. Those walks with you, and I may say that other gentleman's talk, and then that long kind letter I had from you, not signed in your name, and written from abroad—all these changed me, as the child is changed at unrse."

"You have evidently read a good deal since we parted."

"Yes; I belong to our young men's library and institute; and when of an evening I get hold of a book, especially a pleasant story book, I don't care for other company."

"Have you never seen any other girl you could care for, and wish to marry?"

"Ah, sir," answered Tom, "a man does not go so mad for a girl as I did for Jessie Wiles, and when it is all over, and he has come to his senses, put his heart into joint again as easily as if it were only a broken leg. I don't say that I may not live to love and to marry another woman—it is my wish to do so. But I know that I shall love Jessie to my dying day; but not sinfully, sir—not sinfully. I would not wrong her by a thought."

There was a long pause.

At last Kenelm said—"You promised to be kind to that little girl with the flower-ball; what has become of her?"

"She is quite well, thank you, sir. My aunt

has taken a great fancy to her, and so has my mother. She comes to them very often of an evening, and brings her work with her. A quick, intelligent little thing, and full of pretty thoughts. On Sundays, if the weather is fine, we stroll out together in the fields."

"She has been a comfort to you, Tom."

"Oh yes."

"And loves you?"

"I am sure she does; an affectionate, grateful child."

"She will be a woman soon, Tom, and may love you as a woman then."

Tom looked indignant and rather scornful at that suggestion, and hastened to revert to the subject more immediately at his heart.

"Miss Travers said you would like to call on Will Somers and his wife; will you? Moleswich is not far from London, you know."

"Certainly, I will call."

"I do hope you will find them happy; and if so, perhaps you will kindly let me know; and—and—I wonder whether Jessie's child is like her?

It is a boy—somehow or other I would rather it had been a girl."

"I will write you full particulars. But why not come with me?"

"No, I don't think I could do that, just at present. It unsettled me sadly when I did again see her sweet face at Graveleigh, and she was still afraid of me too!—that was a sharp pang."

"She ought to know what you have done for her, and will."

"On no account, sir; promise me that. I should feel mean if I humbled them—that way."

"I understand, though I will not as yet make you any positive promise. Meanwhile, if you are staying in town, lodge with me; my landlady can find you a room."

"Thank you heartily, sir; but I go back by the evening train; and, bless me! how late it is now. I must wish you good-bye. I have some commissions to do for my aunt, and I must buy a new doll for Susey."

"Susey is the name of the little girl with the flower-ball?"

"Yes. I must run off now; I feel quite light at heart seeing you again and finding that you receive me still so kindly, as if we were equals."

"Ah, Tom, I wish I was your equal—nay, half as noble as heaven has made you."

Tom laughed incredulously, and went his way.

"This mischievous passion of love," said Kenelm to himself, "has its good side, it seems, after all. If it was nearly making a wild beast of that brave fellow—nay, worse than wild beast, a homicide doomed to the gibbet—so, on the other hand, what a refined, delicate, chivalrous nature of gentleman it has developed out of the stormy elements of its first madness. Yes, I will go and look at this new-married couple. I dare-say they are already snarling and spitting at each other like cat and dog. Moleswich is within reach of a walk."

BOOK V.

CHAPTER I.

Two days after the interview recorded in the last chapter of the previous Book, Travers, chancing to call at Kenelm's lodgings, was told by his servant that Mr. Chillingly had left London, alone, and had given no orders as to forwarding letters. The servant did not know where he had gone, or when he would return.

Travers repeated this news incidentally to Cecilia, and she felt somewhat hurt that he had not written her a line respecting Tom's visit. She, however, guessed that he had gone to see the Somerses, and would return to town in a day or so. But weeks passed, the season drew to its close, and of Kenelm Chillingly she saw or heard nothing: he had wholly vanished from the London world. He had but written a line to his servant, ordering him to repair to Exmundham and await him there, and enclosing him a cheque to pay outstanding bills.

We must now follow the devious steps of the strange being who has grown into the hero of this story. He had left his apartment at daybreak long before his servant was up, with his knapsack, and a small portmanteau, into which he had thrust—besides such additional articles of dress as he thought he might possibly require, and which his knapsack could not contain—a few of his favourite books. Driving with these in a hack-cab to the Vauxhall station, he directed the portmanteau to be forwarded to Moleswich, and flinging the knapsack on his shoulders, walked slowly along the drowsy suburbs that stretched far into the landscape, before, breathing more freely, he found some evidences of rural culture on either side of the high-road. It was not, however, till he had left the roofs and trees of pleasant Richmond far behind him that he began to feel he was out of reach of the metropolitan disquieting influences. Finding at a little inn, where he stopped to breakfast, that there was a path along fields and in sight of the river, through which he could gain the place of his destination, he then quitted the high-road, and, traversing one of the loveliest districts in one of our loveliest counties, he reached Moleswich about mid-noon.

CHAPTER II.

On entering the main street of the pretty town, the name of Somers, in gilt capitals, was sufficiently conspicuous over the door of a very imposing shop. It boasted two plate-glass windows, at one of which were tastefully exhibited various articles of fine stationery, embroidery patterns, &c.; at the other, no less tastefully, sundry specimens of ornamental basket-work.

Kenelm crossed the threshold and recognised behind the counter—fair as ever, but with an expression of face more staid, and a figure more rounded and matron-like—his old friend Jessie. There were two or three customers before her, between whom she was dividing her attention. While a handsome young lady, seated, was saying, in a somewhat loud, but cheery and pleasant voice, "Do not mind me, Mrs. Somers—I can wait," Jessie's quick eye darted towards the stranger, but too rapidly to distinguish his features, which, indeed, he turned away, and began to examine the baskets.

In a minute or so the other customers were served and had departed. And the voice of the lady was again heard—"Now, Mrs. Somers, I want to see your picture-books and toys. I am giving a little children's party this afternoon, and I want to make them as happy as possible."

"Somewhere or other on this planet, or before my Monad was whisked away to it, I have heard that voice," muttered Kenelm. While Jessie was alertly bringing forth her toys and picture-books, she said, "I am sorry to keep you waiting, sir; but if it is the baskets you come about, I can call my husband."

"Do," said Kenelm.

"William—William," cried Mrs. Somers; and after a delay long enough to allow him to slip on his jacket, William Somers emerged from the back parlour.

His face had lost its old trace of suffering and ill health; it was still somewhat pale, and retained its expression of intellectual refinement.

"How you have improved in your art!" said Kenelm, heartily.

William started, and recognised Kenelm at once. He sprang forward and took Kenelm's outstretched hand in both his own, and, in a voice between laughing and crying, exclaimed—"Jessie, Jessie, it is he!—he whom we pray for every night. God bless you!—God bless and make you as happy as He permitted you to make me!"

Before this little speech was faltered out, Jessie was by her husband's side, and she added, in a lower voice, but tremulous with deep feeling—"And me too!"

"By your leave, Will," said Kenelm, and he saluted Jessie's white forehead with a kiss that could not have been kindlier or colder if it had been her grandfather's.

Meanwhile the lady had risen noiselessly and unobserved, and stealing up to Kenelm, looked him full in the face.

"You have another friend here, sir, who has also some cause to thank you——"

"I thought I remembered your voice," said Kenelm, looking puzzled. "But pardon me if I cannot recall your features. Where have we met before?"

"Give me your arm when we go out, and I will bring myself to your recollection. But no: I must not hurry you away now. I will call again in half an hour. Mrs. Somers, meanwhile put up the things I have selected. I will take them away with me when I come back from the vicarage, where I have left the pony carriage." So, with a parting nod and smile to Kenelm, she turned away, and left him bewildered.

"But who is that lady, Will?"

"A Mrs. Braefield. She is a new-comer."

"She may well be that, Will," said Jessie, smiling, "for she has only been married six months."

"And what was her name before she married."

"I am sure I don't know, sir. It is only

three months since we came here, and she has been very kind to us, and an excellent customer. Everybody likes her. Mr. Braefield is a city gentleman, and very rich; and they live in the finest house in the place, and see a great deal of company."

"Well, I am no wiser than I was before," said Kenelm. "People who ask questions very seldom are."

"And how did you find us out, sir?" said Jessie. "Oh! I guess," she added, with an arch glance and smile. "Of course, you have seen Miss Travers, and she told you."

"You are right. I first learned your change of residence from her, and thought I would come and see you, and be introduced to the baby—a boy, I understand? Like you, Will?"

"No, sir—the picture of Jessie."

"Nonsense, Will; it is you all over, even to its little hands."

"And your good mother, Will, how did you leave her?"

"Oh sir!" cried Jessie reproachfully; "do

you think we could have the heart to leave mother—so lone and rheumatic too? She is tending baby now—always does while I am in the shop."

Here Kenelm followed the young couple into the parlour, where, seated by the window, they found old Mrs. Somers reading the Bible and rocking the baby, who slept peacefully in its cradle.

"Will," said Kenelm, bending his dark face over the infant, "I will tell you a pretty thought of a foreign poet's, which has been thus badly translated:—

"Blest babe, a boundless world this bed so narrow seems
to thee;
Grow man, and narrower than this bed the boundless world
shall be."*

"I don't think that is true sir," said Will, simply; "for a happy home is a world wide enough for any man."

Tears started into Jessie's eyes; she bent down and kissed—not the baby—but the cradle.

* Schiller.

"Will made it." She added, blushing, "I mean the cradle, sir."

Time flew past while Kenelm talked with Will and the old mother, for Jessie was soon summoned back to the shop; and Kenelm was startled when he found the half-hour's grace allowed to him was over, and Jessie put her head in at the door and said, "Mrs. Braefield is waiting for you."

"Good-bye, Will; I shall come and see you again soon; and my mother gives me a commission to buy I don't know how many specimens of your craft."

CHAPTER III.

A SMART pony-phaeton, with a box for a driver in livery equally smart, stood at the shop door.

"Now, Mr. Chillingly," said Mrs. Braefield, "it is my turn to run away with you; get in!"

"Eh!" murmured Kenelm, gazing at her with large dreamy eyes. "Is it possible?"

"Quite possible; get in. Coachman, home! Yes, Mr. Chillingly, you meet again that giddy creature whom you threatened to thrash; it would have served her right. I ought to feel so ashamed to recall myself to your recollection, and yet I am not a bit ashamed. I am proud to show you that I have turned out a steady, respectable woman, and, my husband tells me, a good wife."

"You have only been six months married, I hear," said Kenelm drily. "I hope your husband will say the same six years hence."

"He will say the same sixty years hence, if we live as long."

"How old is he now?"

"Thirty-eight."

"When a man wants only two years of his hundredth, he probably has learned to know his own mind; but then, in most cases, very little mind is left to him to know."

"Don't be satirical, sir; and don't talk as if you were railing at marriage, when you have just left as happy a young couple as the sun ever shone upon; and owing—for Mrs. Somers has told me all about her marriage—owing their happiness to you."

"Their happiness to me! not in the least. I helped them to marry, and in spite of marriage, they helped each other to be happy."

"You are still unmarried yourself?"

"Yes, thank Heaven!"

"And are you happy?"

"No; I can't make myself happy—myself is a discontented brute."

"Then why do you say 'thank Heaven'?"

"Because it is a comfort to think I am not making somebody else unhappy."

"Do you believe that if you loved a wife who loved you, you should make her unhappy?"

"I am sure I don't know; but I have not seen a woman whom I could love as a wife. And we need not push our inquiries further. What has become of that ill-treated grey cob?"

"He was quite well, thank you, when I last heard of him."

"And the uncle who would have inflicted me upon you, if you had not so gallantly defended yourself?"

"He is living where he did live, and has married his housekeeper. He felt a delicate scruple against taking that step till I was married myself, and out of the way."

Here Mrs. Braefield, beginning to speak very hurriedly, as women who seek to disguise emotion often do, informed Kenelm how unhappy she had felt for weeks after having found an asylum with her aunt—how she had been stung by remorse and oppressed by a sense of humiliation at the thought of her folly and the odious recollection of Mr. Compton—how she had declared to herself that she would never marry any one now—never! How Mr. Braefield happened to be on a visit in the neighbourhood, and saw her at church—how he had sought an introduction to her—and how at first she rather disliked him than not; but he was so good and so kind, and when at last he proposed —and she had frankly told him all about her girlish flight and infatuation—how generously he had thanked her for a candour which had placed her as high in his esteem as she had been before in his love. "And from that moment," said Mrs. Braefield, passionately, "my whole heart leapt to him. And now you know all. And here we are at the Lodge."

The pony-phaeton went with great speed up a broad gravel-drive, bordered with rare evergreens, and stopped at a handsome house with a portico in front, and a long conservatory at the garden side—one of those houses which belong to "city gentlemen," and often contain more comfort and exhibit more luxury than many a stately manorial mansion.

Mrs. Braefield evidently felt some pride as she led Kenelm through the handsome hall, paved with Malvern tiles and adorned with Scagliola columns, and into a drawing-room furnished with much taste, and opening on a spacious flower-garden.

"But where is Mr. Braefield?" asked Kenelm.

"Oh, he has taken the rail to his office; but he will be back long before dinner, and of course you dine with us."

"You are very hospitable, but——"

"No buts; I will take no excuse. Don't fear that you shall have only mutton-chops and a rice-pudding; and besides, I have a children's party coming at two o'clock, and there will be all sorts of fun. You are fond of children, I am sure?"

"I rather think I am not. But I have never clearly ascertained my own inclinations upon that subject."

"Well, you shall have ample opportunity to

do so to-day. And oh! I promise you the sight of the loveliest face that you can picture to yourself when you think of your future wife."

"My future wife, I hope, is not yet born," said Kenelm wearily, and with much effort suppressing a yawn. "But, at all events, I will stay till after two o'clock; for two o'clock, I presume, means luncheon."

Mrs. Braefield laughed.—"You retain your appetite."

"Most single men do, provided they don't fall in love and become doubled up."

At this abominable attempt at a pun, Mrs. Braefield disdained to laugh; but turning away from its perpetrator, she took off her hat and gloves and passed her hands lightly over her forehead, as if to smooth back some vagrant tress in locks already sufficiently sheen and trim. She was not quite so pretty in female attire as she had appeared in boy's dress, nor did she look quite as young. In all other respects she was wonderfully improved. There was a serener, a more settled intelligence in her frank bright eyes, a milder expression in the play of her parted lips. Kenelm gazed at her with pleased admiration. And as now, turning from the glass, she encountered his look, a deeper colour came into the clear delicacy of her cheeks, and the frank eyes moistened. She came up to him as he sate, and took his hand in both hers, pressing it warmly, "Ah, Mr. Chillingly," she said, with impulsive tremulous tones, "look round, look round this happy peaceful home!—the life so free from a care, the husband whom I so love and honour; all the blessings that I might have so recklessly lost for ever had I not met with you, had I been punished as I deserved. How often I thought of your words, that 'you would be proud of my friendship when we met again.' What strength they gave me in my hours of humbled self-reproach." Her voice here died away as if in the effort to suppress a sob.

She released his hand, and before he could answer, passed quickly through the open sash into the garden.

CHAPTER IV.

THE children have come,—some thirty of them, pretty as English children generally are, happy in the joy of the summer sunshine, and the flower lawns, and the feast under cover of an awning suspended between chestnut trees, and carpeted with sward.

No doubt Kenelm held his own at the banquet, and did his best to increase the general gaiety, for whenever he spoke the children listened eagerly, and when he had done they laughed mirthfully.

"The fair face I promised you," whispered Mrs. Braefield, "is not here yet. I have a little note from the young lady to say that Mrs. Cameron does not feel very well this morning, but hopes to recover sufficiently to come later in the afternoon."

"And pray who is Mrs. Cameron?"

"Ah! I forgot that you are a stranger to the place. Mrs. Cameron is the aunt with whom Lily resides. Is it not a pretty name, Lily?"

"Very! emblematic of a spinster that does not spin, with a white head and a thin stalk."

"Then the name belies my Lily, as you will see."

The children now finished their feast, and betook themselves to dancing in an alley smoothed for a croquet ground, and to the sound of a violin played by the old grandfather of one of the party. While Mrs. Braefield was busying herself with forming the dance, Kenelm seized the occasion to escape from a young nymph of the age of twelve who had sat next him at the banquet, and taken so great a fancy to him that he began to fear she would vow never to forsake his side, and stole away undetected.

There are times when the mirth of others only saddens us, especially the mirth of children with high spirits, that jar on our own quiet mood. Gliding through a dense shrubbery in which, though the lilacs were faded, the laburnum still retained here and there the waning gold of its clusters, Kenelm came into a recess which bounded his steps and invited him to repose. It was a circle, so formed artificially by slight trellices, to which clung parasite roses heavy with leaves and flowers. In the midst played a tiny fountain with a silvery murmuring sound; at the background, dominating the place, rose the crests of stately trees on which the sunlight shimmered, but which rampired out all horizon beyond. Even as in life do the great dominant passions—love, ambition, desire of power, or gold, or fame, or knowledge—form the proud background to the brief-lived flowerets of our youth, lift our eyes beyond the smile of their bloom, catch the glint of a loftier sunbeam, and yet, and yet, exclude our sight from the lengths and the widths of the space which extends behind and beyond them.

Kenelm threw himself on the turf beside the fountain. From afar came the whoop and the laugh of the children in their sports or their dance. At the distance their joy did not sadden him—he marvelled why; and thus, in musing reverie, thought to explain the why to himself.

"The poet," so ran his lazy thinking, "has told us that 'distance lends enchantment to the view,' and thus compares to the charm of distance the illusion of hope. But the poet narrows the scope of his own illustration. Distance lends enchantment to the ear as well as to the sight; nor to these bodily senses alone. Memory no less than hope owes its charm to 'the far away.'

"I cannot imagine myself again a child when I am in the midst of yon noisy children. But as their noise reaches me here, subdued and mellowed, and knowing, thank heaven! that the urchins are not within reach of me, I could readily dream myself back into childhood, and into sympathy with the lost playfields of school.

"So surely it must be with grief: how different the terrible agony for a beloved one just gone from earth, to the soft regret for one who disappeared into heaven years ago! So with the art of poetry: how imperatively, when it deals with the great emotions of tragedy, it must remove the actors from us, in proportion as the emotions are to elevate, and the tragedy is to please us by the tears it draws! Imagine our shock if a poet were to place on the stage some wise gentleman with whom we dined yesterday, and who was discovered to have killed his father and married his mother. But when Œdipus commits those unhappy mistakes nobody is shocked. Oxford in the nineteenth century is a long way off from Thebes 3000 or 4000 years ago.

"And," continued Kenelm, plunging deeper into the maze of metaphysical criticism, "even where the poet deals with persons and things close upon our daily sight—if he would give them poetic charm he must resort to a sort of moral or psychological distance; the nearer they are to us in external circumstance, the farther they must be in some internal peculiarities. Werter and Clarissa Harlowe are described as contemporaries of their artistic creation, and with the minutest details of an apparent realism; yet they are at once removed from our daily lives by their idiosyncrasies and their fates. We know that while Werter and Clarissa are so near to us in much that we sympathise with them as friends and kinsfolk, they are yet as much remote from us in the poetic and idealised side of their natures as if they belonged to the age of Homer; and this it is that invests with charm the very pain which their fate inflicts on us. Thus, I suppose, it must be in love. If the love we feel is to have the glamour of poetry, it must be love for some one morally at a distance from our ordinary habitual selves; in short, differing from us in attributes which, however near we draw to the possessor, we can never approach, never blend, in attributes of our own; so that there is something in the loved one that always remains an ideal—a mystery—'a sun-bright summit mingling with the sky!'"

Herewith the soliloquist's musings slided vaguely into mere reverie. He closed his eyes drowsily, not asleep nor yet quite awake: as sometimes in bright summer days when we recline on the grass we do close our eyes, and yet dimly recognise a golden light bathing the drowsy lids; and athwart that light images come and go like dreams, though we know that we are not dreaming.

CHAPTER V.

From this state, half-comatose, half-unconscious, Kenelm was roused slowly, reluctantly. Something struck softly on his cheek—again a little less softly; he opened his eyes—they fell first upon two tiny rosebuds, which, on striking his face, had fallen on his breast; and then, looking up, he saw before him in an opening of the trelliced circle a female child's laughing face. Her hand was still uplifted charged with another rosebud, but, behind the child's figure; looking over her shoulder and holding back the menacing arm, was a face as innocent but lovelier far—the face of a girl in her first youth, framed round with the blossoms that festooned the trellice. How the face became the flowers! It seemed the fairy spirit of them.

Kenelm started and rose to his feet. The child, the one whom he had so ungallantly escaped from, ran towards him through a wicket in the circle. Her companion disappeared.

"Is it you?" said Kenelm to the child—"you who pelted me so cruelly? Ungrateful creature! Did I not give you the best strawberries in the dish and all my own cream?"

"But why did you run away and hide yourself when you ought to be dancing with me," replied the young lady, evading, with the instinct of her sex, all answer to the reproach she had deserved.

"I did not run away, and it is clear that I did not mean to hide myself since you so easily found me out. But who was the young lady with you; I suspect she pelted me too, for *she* seems to have run away to hide herself."

"No, she did not pelt you; she wanted to stop me, and you would have had another rosebud—oh, so much bigger—if she had not held back my arm. Don't you know her—don't you know Lily?"

"No; so that is Lily? You shall introduce me to her."

By this time they had passed out of the circle

through the little wicket opposite the path by which Kenelm had entered, and opening at once on the lawn. Here at some distance the children were grouped, some reclined on the grass, some walking to and fro, in the interval of the dance.

In the space between the group and the trellice, Lily was walking alone and quickly. The child left Kenelm's side and ran after her friend, soon overtook, but did not succeed in arresting her steps. Lily did not pause till she had reached the grassy ball-room, and here all the children came round her and shut out her delicate form from Kenelm's sight.

Before he had reached the place, Mrs. Braefield met him.

"Lily is come!"

"I know it—I have seen her."

"Is not she beautiful?"

"I must see more of her if I am to answer critically; but before you introduce me, may I be permitted to ask who and what is Lily."

Mrs. Braefield paused a moment before she answered, and yet the answer was brief enough not to need much consideration. "She is a Miss Mordaunt, an orphan; and, as I before told you, resides with her aunt, Mrs. Cameron, a widow. They have the prettiest cottage you ever saw on the banks of the river, or rather rivulet, about a mile from this place. Mrs. Cameron is a very good, simple-hearted woman. As to Lily, I can praise her beauty only with safe conscience, for as yet she is a mere child—her mind quite unformed."

"Did you ever meet any man, much less any woman, whose mind was formed?" muttered Kenelm. "I am sure mine is not, and never will be on this earth."

Mrs. Braefield did not hear this low-voiced observation. She was looking about for Lily; and perceiving her at last as the children who surrounded her were dispersing to renew the dance, she took Kenelm's arm, led him to the young lady, and a formal introduction took place.

Formal as it could be on those sunlit swards, amidst the joy of summer and the laugh of children. In such scene and such circumstance, formality does not last long. I know not how it was, but in a very few minutes Kenelm and Lily had ceased to be strangers to each other. They found themselves seated apart from the rest of the merry-makers, on a bank shadowed by lime-trees; the man listening with downcast eyes, the girl with mobile shifting glances now on earth now on heaven, and talking freely, gaily—like the babble of a happy stream, with a silvery dulcet voice, and a sparkle of rippling smiles.

No doubt this is a reversal of the formalities of well-bred life, and conventional narrating thereof. According to them, no doubt, it is for the man to talk and the maid to listen; but I state the facts as they were, honestly. And Lily knew no more of the formalities of drawing-room life than a skylark fresh from its nest knows of the song-teacher and the cage. She was still so much of a child. Mrs. Braefield was right—her mind was still so unformed.

What she did talk about in that first talk between them that could make the meditative Kenelm listen so mutely, so intently I know not, at least I could not jot it down on paper. I fear it was very egotistical, as the talk of children generally is—about herself and her aunt, and her home and her friends—all her friends seemed children like herself, though younger—Clemmy the chief of them. Clemmy was the one who had taken a fancy to Kenelm. And amidst all this ingenuous prattle there came flashes of a quick intellect, a lively fancy—nay, even a poetry of expression or of sentiment. It might be the talk of a child, but certainly not of a silly child.

But as soon as the dance was over, the little ones again gathered round Lily. Evidently she was the prime favourite of them all; and as her companion had now become tired of dancing, new sports were proposed, and Lily was carried off to "Prisoner's Bass."

"I am very happy to make your acquaintance, Mr. Chillingly," said a frank, pleasant voice; and a well-dressed, good-looking man held out his hand to Kenelm.

"My husband," said Mrs. Braefield, with a certain pride in her look.

Kenelm responded cordially to the civilities of the master of the house, who had just returned from his city office, and left all its cares behind him. You had only to look at him to see that he was prosperous, and deserved to be so. There were in his countenance the signs of strong sense, of good-humour—above all, of an active energetic temperament. A man of broad smooth forehead, keen hazel eyes, firm lips and jaw; with a happy contentment in himself, his house, the world in general, mantling over his genial smile, and out-spoken in the metallic ring of his voice.

"You will stay and dine with us, of course," said Mr. Braefield; "and unless you want very much to be in town to-night, I hope you will take a bed here."

Kenelm hesitated.

"Do stay at least till to-morrow," said Mrs. Braefield. Kenelm hesitated still; and while hesitating his eye rested on Lily, leaning on the arm of a middle-aged lady, and approaching the hostess—evidently to take leave.

"I cannot resist so tempting an invitation,"

said Kenelm, and he fell back a little behind Lily and her companion.

"Thank you much for so pleasant a day," said Mrs. Cameron to the hostess. "Lily has enjoyed herself extremely. I only regret we could not come earlier."

"If you are walking home," said Mr. Braefield, "let me accompany you. I want to speak to your gardener about his heartsease—it is much finer than mine."

"If so," said Kenelm to Lily, "may I come too? Of all flowers that grow, heartsease is the one I most prize."

A few minutes afterwards Kenelm was walking by the side of Lily along the banks of a little stream, tributary to the Thames—Mrs. Cameron and Mr. Braefield in advance, for the path only held two abreast.

Suddenly Lily left his side, allured by a rare butterfly—I think it is called the Emperor of Morocco—that was sunning its yellow wings upon a group of wild reeds. She succeeded in capturing this wanderer in her straw hat, over which she drew her sunveil. After this notable capture she returned demurely to Kenelm's side.

"Do you collect insects?" said that philosopher, as much surprised as it was his nature to be at anything.

"Only butterflies," answered Lily; "they are not insects, you know; they are souls."

"Emblems of souls you mean—at least, so the Greeks prettily represented them to be."

"No, real souls—the souls of infants that die in their cradles unbaptised; and if they are taken care of, and not eaten by birds, and live a year, then they pass into fairies."

"It is a very poetical idea, Miss Mordaunt, and founded on evidence quite as rational as other assertions of the metamorphosis of one creature into another. Perhaps you can do what the philosophers cannot—tell me how you learned a new idea to be an incontestible fact?"

"I don't know," replied Lily, looking very

much puzzled; "perhaps I learned it in a book, or perhaps I dreamed it."

"You could not make a wiser answer if you were a philosopher. But you talk of taking care of butterflies; how do you do that? Do you impale them on pins stuck into a glass case?"

"Impale them! How can you talk so cruelly? You deserve to be pinched by the Fairies."

"I am afraid," thought Kenelm, compassionately, "that my companion has no mind to be formed; what is euphoniously called 'an Innocent.'"

He shook his head and remained silent.

Lily resumed—

"I will show you my collection when we get home--they seem so happy. I am sure there are some of them who know me—they will feed from my hand. I have only had one die since I began to collect them last summer."

"Then you have kept them a year; they ought to have turned into fairies."

"I suppose many of them have. Of course I let out all those that had been with me twelve months--they don't turn to fairies in the cage, you know. Now I have only those I caught this year, or last autumn; the prettiest don't appear till the autumn."

The girl here bent her uncovered head over the straw hat, her tresses shadowing it, and uttered loving words to the prisoner. Then again she looked up and around her, and abruptly stopped, and exclaimed—

"How can people live in towns—how can people say they are ever dull in the country? Look," she continued, gravely and earnestly—"look at that tall pine tree, with its long branch sweeping over the water; see how, as the breeze catches it, it changes its shadow, and how the shadow changes the play of the sunlight on the brook:—

> 'Wave your tops, ye pines;
> With every plant, in sign of worship wave.'

What an interchange of music there must be between Nature and a poet!"

Kenelm was startled. This "an innocent"! —this a girl who had no mind to be formed!

In that presence he could not be cynical; could not speak of Nature as a mechanism, a lying humbug; as he had done to the man poet. He replied gravely—

"The Creator has gifted the whole universe with language, but few are the hearts that can interpret it. Happy those to whom it is no foreign tongue, acquired imperfectly with care and pain, but rather a native language, learned unconsciously from the lips of the great mother. To them the butterfly's wing may well buoy into heaven a fairy's soul!"

When he had thus said Lily turned, and for the first time attentively looked into his dark soft eyes; then instinctively she laid her light hand on his arm, and said in a low voice, "Talk on—talk thus; I like to hear you."

But Kenelm did not talk on. They had now arrived at the garden gate of Mrs. Cameron's cottage, and the elder persons in advance paused at the gate and walked with them to the house.

It was a long low irregular cottage, without

pretension to architectural beauty, yet exceedingly picturesque—a flower-garden, large but in proportion to the house, with parterres in which the colours were exquisitely assorted, sloping to the grassy margin of the rivulet, where the stream expanded into a lake-like basin, narrowed at either end by locks, from which with gentle sound flowed shallow waterfalls. By the banks was a rustic seat, half over-shadowed by the dropping boughs of a vast willow.

The inside of the house was in harmony with the exterior—cottage-like, but with an unmistakable air of refinement about the rooms, even in the little entrance hall, which was painted in Pompeian frescoes.

"Come and see my butterfly-cage," said Lily, whisperingly.

Kenelm followed her through the window that opened on the garden; and at one end of a small conservatory, or rather greenhouse, was the habitation of these singular favourites. It was as large as a small room; three sides of it formed by minute wire-work, with occasional draperies of muslin or other slight material, and covered at intervals, sometimes within, sometimes without, by dainty creepers; a tiny cistern in the centre, from which upsprang a sparkling jet. Lily cautiously lifted a sash door and glided in, closing it behind her. Her entrance set in movement a multitude of gossamer wings, some fluttering round her, some more boldly settling on her hair or dress. Kenelm thought she had not vainly boasted when she said that some of the creatures had learned to know her. She relieved the Emperor of Morocco from her hat; it circled round her fearlessly, and then vanished amidst the leaves of the creepers. Lily opened the door and came out.

"I have heard of a philosopher who tamed a wasp," said Kenelm, "but never before of a young lady who tamed butterflies."

"No," said Lily proudly; "I believe I am the first who attempted it. I don't think I should have attempted it if I had been told that others had succeeded before me. Not that I have succeeded quite. No matter; if they don't love me, I love them."

They re-entered the drawing-room, and Mrs. Cameron addressed Kenelm.

"Do you know much of this part of the country, Mr. Chillingly?"

"It is quite new to me, and more rural than many districts further from London."

"That is the good fortune of most of our home counties," said Mr. Braefield; "they escape the smoke and din of manufacturing towns, and agricultural science has not demolished their leafy hedgerows. The walks through our green lanes are as much bordered with convolvulus and honeysuckle as they were when Izaak Walton sauntered through them to angle in that stream!"

"Does tradition say that he angled in that stream? I thought his haunts were rather on the other side of London."

"Possibly; I am not learned in Walton or in his art, but there is an old summer-house, on the other side of the lock yonder, on which is carved the name of Izaak Walton, but whether by his own hand or another's who shall say? Has Mr. Melville been here lately, Mrs. Cameron?"

"No, not for several months."

"He has had a glorious success this year. We may hope that at last his genius is acknowledged by the world. I meant to buy his picture, but I was not in time—a Manchester man was before me."

"Who is Mr. Melville? any relation to you?" whispered Kenelm to Lily.

"Relation!—I scarcely know. Yes, I suppose so, because he is my guardian. But if he were the nearest relation on earth, I could not love him more," said Lily, with impulsive eagerness, her cheeks flushing, her eyes filling with tears.

"And he is an artist—a painter?" asked Kenelm.

"Oh yes; no one paints such beautiful pictures—no one so clever, no one so kind."

Kenelm strove to recollect if he had ever heard the name of Melville as a painter, but in vain. Kenelm, however, knew but little of painters—they were not in his way; and he owned to himself, very humbly, that there might be many a living painter of eminent renown whose name and works would be strange to him.

He glanced round the wall,—Lily interpreted his look. "There are no pictures of his here," said she; "there is one in my own room. I will show it you when you come again."

"And now," said Mr. Braefield, rising, "I must just have a word with your gardener, and then go home. We dine earlier here than in London, Mr. Chillingly."

As the two gentlemen, after taking leave, re-entered the hall, Lily followed them and said to Kenelm, "What time will you come to-morrow to see the picture?"

Kenelm averted his head, and then replied, not with his wonted courtesy, but briefly and brusquely—

"I fear I cannot call to-morrow. I shall be far away by sunrise."

Lily made no answer, but turned back into the room.

Mr. Braefield found the gardener watering a

flower-border, conferred with him about the heartsease, and then joined Kenelm, who had halted a few yards beyond the garden gate.

"A pretty little place that," said Mr. Braefield with a sort of lordly compassion, as became the owner of Braefieldville. "What I call quaint."

"Yes, quaint," echoed Kenelm, abstractedly.

"It is always the case with houses enlarged by degrees. I have heard my poor mother say that when Melville or Mrs. Cameron first bought it, it was little better than a mere labourer's cottage, with a field attached to it. And two or three years afterwards a room or so more was built, and a bit of the field taken in for a garden; and then by degrees the whole part now inhabited by the family was built, leaving only the old cottage as a scullery and wash-house; and the whole field was turned into the garden as you see. But whether it was Melville's money or the aunt's that did it, I don't know. More likely the aunt's. I don't see what interest Melville has in the place; he does not go there often, I fancy—it is not his home."

"Mr. Melville, it seems, is a painter, and, from what I heard you say, a successful one."

"I fancy he had little success before this year. But surely you saw his pictures at the Exhibition?"

"I am ashamed to say I have not been to the Exhibition."

"You surprise me. However, Melville had three pictures there; all very good, but the one I wished to buy made much more sensation than the others, and has suddenly lifted him from obscurity into fame."

"He appears to be a relation of Miss Mordaunt's, but so distant a one, that she could not even tell me what grade of cousinship he could claim."

"Nor can I. He is her guardian, I know. The relationship, if any, must, as you say, be very distant; for Melville is of humble extraction, while any one can see that Mrs. Cameron is a thorough gentlewoman, and Lily Mordaunt is her sister's child. I have heard my mother say that it was Melville, then a very young man, who bought the cottage, perhaps with Mrs. Cameron's money; saying it was for a widowed lady, whose husband had left her with very small means. And when Mrs. Cameron arrived with Lily, then a mere infant, she was in deep mourning, and a very young woman herself,—pretty too. If Melville had been a frequent visitor then, of course there would have been scandal; but he very seldom came, and when he did, he lodged in a cottage, Cromwell Lodge, on the other side of the brook; now and then bringing with him a fellow-lodger—some other young artist, I suppose, for the sake of angling. So there could be no cause for scandal, and nothing can be more blameless than poor Mrs. Cameron's life. My mother, who then resided at Braefieldville, took a great fancy to both Lily and her aunt, and when by degrees the cottage grew into a genteel sort of place, the few gentry in the neighbourhood followed my mother's example and were very kind to Mrs. Cameron, so that she has now her place in the society about here, and is much liked."

"And Mr. Melville?—does he still very seldom come here?"

"To say truth, he has not been at all since I settled at Braefieldville. The place was left to my mother for her life, and I was not much there during her occupation. In fact, I was then a junior partner in our firm, and conducted the branch business in New York, coming over to England for my holiday once a-year or so. When my mother died, there was much to arrange before I could settle personally in England, and I did not come to settle at Braefieldville till I married. I did see Melville on one of my visits to the place some years ago; but, between ourselves, he is not the sort of person whose intimate acquaintance one would wish to court. My mother told me he was an idle, dissipated man, and I have heard from others that he was very unsteady. Mr.——, the great painter, told me that he was a loose fish; and I suppose his habits were against his getting on, till this year, when, perhaps by a lucky accident, he has painted a picture that raises him to the top of the tree. But is not Miss Lily wondrously nice to look at? What a pity her education has been so much neglected."

"Has it?"

"Have not you discovered that already? She has not had even a music-master, though my wife says she has a good ear, and can sing prettily enough. As for reading, I don't think she has read anything but fairy tales and poetry, and such silly stuff. However, she is very young yet; and now that her guardian can sell his pictures, it is to be hoped that he will do more justice to his ward. Painters and actors are not so regular in their private lives as we plain men are, and great allowance is to be made for them; still, every one is bound to do his duty. I am sure you agree with me?"

"Certainly," said Kenelm, with an emphasis which startled the merchant. "That is an admirable maxim of yours: it seems a commonplace, yet how often, when it is put into our heads, it strikes as a novelty. A duty may be a very difficult thing, a very disagreeable thing, and, what is strange, it is often a very invisible thing. It is present—close before us, and yet we don't see it; somebody shouts its name in our ears, 'Duty,' and straight it towers before us a grim giant. Pardon me if I leave you—I can't stay to dine. Duty summons me elsewhere. Make my excuses to Mrs. Braefield."

Before Mr. Braefield could recover his self-possession, Kenelm had vaulted over a stile and was gone.

CHAPTER VI.

KENELM walked into the shop kept by the Somerses, and found Jessie still at the counter. "Give me back my knapsack. Thank you," he said, flinging the knapsack across his shoulders. "Now, do me a favour. A portmanteau of mine ought to be at the station. Send for it, and keep it till I give further directions. I think of going to Oxford for a day or two. Mrs. Somers, one more word with you. Think, answer frankly, are you, as you said this morning, thoroughly happy, and yet married to the man you loved?"

"Oh, so happy!"

"And wish for nothing beyond? Do not wish Will to be other than he is?"

"God forbid! You frighten me, sir."

"Frighten you! Be it so. Every one who is happy should be frightened, lest happiness fly away. Do your best to chain it, and you will, for you attach Duty to Happiness; and," muttered Kenelm, as he turned from the shop, "Duty is sometimes not a rose-coloured tie, but a heavy iron-hued clog."

He strode on through the street towards the sign-post with "To Oxford" inscribed thereon. And whether he spoke literally of the knapsack, or metaphorically of Duty, he murmured, as he strode—

> "A pedlar's pack that bows the bearer down."

CHAPTER VII.

KENELM might have reached Oxford that night, for he was a rapid and untireable pedestrian; but he halted a little after the moon rose, and laid himself down to rest beneath a new-mown haystack, not very far from the high-road.

He did not sleep. Meditatingly propped on his elbow, he said to himself—

"It is long since I have wondered at nothing. I wonder now: can this be love—really love—unmistakeably love? Pooh! it is impossible; the very last person in the world to be in love with. Let us reason upon it—you, myself, and I. To begin with—face! What is face? In a few years the most beautiful face may be very plain. Take the Venus at Florence. Animate her; see her ten years after; a chignon, front teeth (blue or artificially white), mottled complexion, double chin—all that sort of plump prettiness goes into double chin. Face, bah! What man of sense—

what pupil of Welby, the realist—can fall in love with a face? and even if I were simpleton enough to do so, pretty faces are as common as daisies. Cecilia Travers has more regular features; Jessie Wiles a richer colouring. I was not in love with them—not a bit of it. Myself, you have nothing to say there. Well, then, mind? Talk of mind, indeed! a creature whose favourite companionship is that of butterflies, and who tells me that butterflies are the souls of infants unbaptised. What an article for 'The Londoner,' on the culture of young women. What a girl for Miss Garrett and Miss Emily Faithfull! Put aside Mind as we have done Face. What rests?—the Frenchman's ideal of happy marriage? congenial circumstance of birth, fortune, tastes, habits. Worse still. Myself, answer honestly, are you not floored?"

Whereon "Myself" took up the parable and answered—"O thou fool! why wert thou so ineffably blest in one presence? Why, in quitting that presence, did Duty become so grim? Why dost thou address to me those inept pedantic questionings, under the light of yon moon, which has suddenly ceased to be to thy thoughts an astronomical body, and has become, for ever and for ever, identified in thy heart's dreams with romance and poesy and first love? Why, instead of gazing on that uncomfortable orb, art thou not quickening thy steps towards a cozy inn and a good supper at Oxford? Kenelm, my friend, thou art in for it. No disguising the fact—thou art in love!"

"I'll be hanged if I am," said the Second in the Dualism of Kenelm's mind; and therewith he shifted his knapsack into a pillow, turned his eyes from the moon, and still could not sleep. The face of Lily still haunted his eyes—the voice of Lily still rang in his ears.

Oh, my reader! dost thou here ask me to tell thee what Lily was like?—was she dark, was she fair, was she tall, was she short? Never shalt thou learn these secrets from me. Imagine to thyself the being to which thine whole of life, body and mind and soul, moved irresistibly as the needle to the pole. Let her be tall or short, dark or fair, she is that which out of all womankind has suddenly become the one woman for thee. Fortunate art thou, my reader, if thou chance to have heard the popular song of "My Queen" sung by the one lady who alone can sing it with expression worthy the verse of the poetess and the music of the composition, by the sister of the exquisite songstress. But if thou hast not heard the verse thus sung, to an accompaniment thus composed, still the words themselves are, or ought to be, familiar to thee, if thou art, as I take for granted, a lover of the true lyrical muse. Recall then the words supposed to be uttered by him who knows himself destined to do homage to one he has not yet beheld:—

"She is standing somewhere—she I shall honour,
She that I wait for, my queen, my queen;
Whether her hair be golden or raven,
Whether her eyes be hazel or blue,
I know not now, it will be engraven
Some day hence as my loveliest hue.

"She may be humble or proud, my lady,
Or that sweet calm which is just between;
But whenever she comes, she will find me ready
To do her homage, my queen, my queen."

Was it possible that the cruel boy-god "who sharpens his arrows on the whetstone of the human heart" had found the moment to avenge himself for the neglect of his altars and the scorn of his power. Must that redoubted knight-errant, the hero of this tale, despite The Three Fishes on his charmed shield, at last veil the crest and bow the knee, and murmur to himself, "She has come, my queen!"

CHAPTER VIII.

THE next morning Kenelm arrived at Oxford —"Verum secretumque Mouseion."

If there be a place in this busy island which may distract the passions of youth from love to scholarship, to Ritualism, to mediæval associations, to that sort of poetical sentiment or poetical fanaticism which a Mivers and a Welby and an advocate of the Realistic School would hold in contempt—certainly that place is Oxford. Home, nevertheless, of great thinkers and great actors in the practical world.

The vacation had not yet commenced, but the commencement was near at hand. Kenelm thought he could recognise the leading men by their slower walk and more abstracted expression of countenance. Among the fellows was the eminent author of that book which had so powerfully fascinated the earlier adolescence of Kenelm Chillingly, and who had himself been subject to the fascination of a yet stronger spirit. The Rev. Decimus Roach had been ever an intense and reverent admirer of John Henry Newman—an admirer, I mean of the pure and lofty character of the man, quite apart from sympathy with his doctrines. But although Roach remained an unconverted Protestant of orthodox, if High Church, creed, yet there was one tenet he did hold in common with the author of the 'Apologia.' He ranked celibacy among the virtues most dear to Heaven. In that eloquent treatise, 'The Approach to the Angels,' he not only maintained that the state of single blessedness was strictly incumbent on every member of a Christian priesthood, but to be commended to the adoption of every conscientious layman.

It was the desire to confer with this eminent theologian that had induced Kenelm to direct his steps to Oxford.

Mr. Roach was a friend of Welby's, at whose house, when a pupil, Kenelm had once or twice met him, and been even more charmed by his conversation than by his treatise. Kenelm called on Mr. Roach, who received him very graciously, and not being a tutor or examiner, placed his time at Kenelm's disposal; took him the round of the colleges and the Bodleian; invited him to dine in his college-hall; and after dinner led him into his own rooms, and gave him an excellent bottle of Chateau Margaux.

Mr. Roach was somewhere about fifty—a good-looking man, and evidently thought himself so, for he wore his hair long behind and parted in the middle; which is not done by men who form modest estimates of their personal appearance.

Kenelm was not long in drawing out his host on the subject to which that profound thinker had devoted so much meditation.

"I can scarcely convey to you," said Kenelm, "the intense admiration with which I have studied your noble work, 'Approach to the Angels.' It produced a great effect on me in the age between boyhood and youth. But of late some doubts on the universal application of your doctrine have crept into my mind."

"Ay, indeed?" said Mr. Roach, with an expression of interest in his face.

"And I come to you for their solution."

Mr. Roach turned away his head, and pushed the bottle to Kenelm.

"I am quite willing to concede," resumed the heir of the Chillinglys, "that a priesthood should stand apart from the distracting cares of a family, and pure from all carnal affections."

"Hem, hem," grunted Mr. Roach, taking his knee on his lap and caressing it.

"I go farther," continued Kenelm, "and supposing with you that the Confessional has all the importance, whether in its monitory or its cheering effects upon repentant sinners, which is attached to it by the Roman Catholics, and that it ought to be no less cultivated by the Reformed Church, it seems to me essential that the Confessor should have no better half to whom it can be even suspected he may, in an unguarded moment, hint at the frailties of one of her female acquaintances."

"I pushed that argument too far," murmured Roach.

"Not a bit of it. Celibacy in the Confessor stands or falls with the Confessional. Your argument there is as sound as a bell. But when it comes to the layman, I think I detect a difference."

Mr. Roach shook his head, and replied stoutly, "No; if celibacy be incumbent on the one, it is equally incumbent on the other. I say 'if'."

"Permit me to deny that assertion. Do not fear that I shall insult your understanding by the popular platitude—viz., that if celibacy were universal, in a very few years the human race would be extinct. As you have justly observed, in answer to that fallacy, 'It is the duty of each human soul to strive towards the highest perfection of the spiritual state for itself, and leave the fate of the human race to the care of the Creator.' If celibacy be necessary to spiritual perfection, how do we know but that it may be the purpose and decree of the All Wise that the human race, having attained to that perfection, should disappear from earth. Universal celibacy would thus be the euthanasia of mankind. On the other hand, if the Creator decided that the human race, having culminated to this crowning but barren flower of perfection, should nevertheless continue to increase and multiply upon earth, have you not victoriously exclaimed, 'Presumptuous mortal! how canst thou presume to limit the resources of the Almighty? Would it not be easy for Him to continue some other mode, unexposed to trouble and sin and passion, as in the nuptials of the vegetable world, by which the generations will be renewed! Can we suppose that the angels—the immortal companies of heaven—are not hourly increasing in number, and extending their populations throughout infinity? and yet in heaven there is no marrying nor giving in marriage'.—All this, clothed by you in words which my memory only serves me to quote imperfectly—all this I unhesitatingly concede."

Mr. Roach rose and brought another bottle of the Chateau Margaux from his cellaret, filled Kenelm's glass, reseated himself, and took the other knee into his lap to caress.

"But," resumed Kenelm, "my doubt is this."

"Ha!" cried Mr. Roach, "let us hear the doubt."

"In the first place, is celibacy essential to the highest state of spiritual perfection? and in the second place, if it were, are mortals, as at present constituted, capable of that culmination?"

"Very well put," said Mr. Roach, and he tossed off his glass with more cheerful aspect than he had hitherto exhibited.

"You see," said Kenelm, "we are compelled in this, as in other questions of philosophy, to resort to the inductive process, and draw our theories from the facts within our cognizance. Now, looking round the world, is it the fact that old maids and old bachelors are so much more spiritually advanced than married folks? Do they pass their time, like an Indian dervish, in serene contemplation of divine excellence and beatitude? Are they not quite as worldly in their own way as persons who have been married as often as the Wife of Bath, and, generally speaking, more selfish, more frivolous, and more spiteful? I am sure I don't wish to speak uncharitably against old maids and old bachelors. I have three aunts who are old maids, and fine specimens of the genus; but I am sure they would all three have been more agreeable companions, and quite as spiritually gifted, if they had been happily married, and were caressing their children instead of lap-dogs. So, too, I have an old bachelor-cousin, Chillingly Mivers, whom you know. As clever as a man can be. But, Lord bless you! as to being wrapt in spiritual meditation, he could not be more devoted to the things of earth if he had married as many wives as Solomon, and had as many children as Priam. Finally, have not half the mistakes in the world arisen from a separation between the spiritual and the moral nature of man? Is it not, after all, through his dealings with his fellow-men that man makes his safest 'approach to the angels'? And is not the moral system a very muscular system? Does it not require for healthful vigour plenty of continued exercise, and does it not get that exercise naturally, by the relationships of family, with all the wider collateral struggles with life which the care of family necessitates?

"I put these questions to you with the humblest diffidence. I expect to hear such answers as will thoroughly convince my reason, and I shall be delighted if so. For at the root of the controversy lies the passion of love. And love must be a very disquieting troublesome emotion, and has led many heroes and sages into wonderful weaknesses and follies."

"Gently, gently, Mr. Chillingly; don't exaggerate. Love, no doubt, is—ahem—a disquieting passion. Still every emotion that changes life from a stagnant pool into the freshness and play of a running stream is disquieting to the pool. Not only love and its fellow-passions—such as ambition—but the exercise of the reasoning faculty, which is always at work in changing our ideas, is very disquieting. Love, Mr. Chillingly, has its good side as well as its bad. Pass the bottle."

Kenelm (passing the bottle).—"Yes, yes; you are quite right in putting the adversary's case strongly before you demolish it—all good rhetoricians do that. Pardon me if I am up to that trick in argument. Assume that I know all that can be said in favour of the abnegation of common-sense, euphoniously called 'love,' and proceed to the demolition of the case."

The Rev. Decimus Roach (hesitatingly).—"The demolition of the case? humph! The passions are ingrafted in the human system as part and parcel of it, and are not to be demolished so easily as you seem to think. Love, taken rationally and morally by a man of good education and sound principles, is—is——"

Kenelm.—"Well, is what?"

The Rev. Decimus Roach.—"A—a—a—thing not to be despised. Like the sun, it is the great colourist of life, Mr. Chillingly. And you are so right—the moral system does require daily exercise. What can give that exercise to a solitary man, when he arrives at the practical age in which he cannot sit for six hours at a stretch musing on the divine essence; and rheumatism or other ailments forbid his adventure into the wilds of Africa as a missionary? At that age, Nature, which will be heard, Mr. Chillingly, demands her rights. A sympathising female companion by one's side; innocent little children climbing one's knee,—lovely, bewitching picture! Who can be Goth enough to rub it out, who fanatic enough to paint over it the image of a St. Simon sitting alone on a pillar! Take another glass. You don't drink enough, Mr. Chillingly."

"I have drunk enough," replied Kenelm, in a sullen voice, "to think I see double. I imagined that before me sate the austere adversary of the insanity of love and the miseries of wedlock. Now, I fancy I listen to a puling sentimentalist uttering the platitudes which the other Decimus Roach had already refuted. Certainly either I see double, or you amuse yourself with mocking my appeal to your wisdom."

"Not so, Mr. Chillingly. But the fact is, that when I wrote that book of which you speak, I was young, and youth is enthusiastic and one-sided. Now, with the same disdain of the excesses to which love may hurry weak intellects, I recognise its benignant effects when taken, as I before said, rationally—taken rationally, my young friend. At that period of life when the judgment is matured, the soothing companionship of an amiable female cannot but cheer the mind, and prevent that morose hoar-frost into which solitude is chilled and made rigid by increasing years. In short, Mr. Chillingly, having convinced myself that I erred in the opinion once too rashly put forth, I owe it to Truth, I owe it to Mankind, to make my conversion known to the world. And I am about next month to enter into the matrimonial state with a young lady who——"

"Say no more, say no more, Mr. Roach. It must be a painful subject to you. Let us drop it."

"It is not a painful subject at all!" exclaimed Mr. Roach, with warmth. "I look forward to the fulfilment of my duty with the pleasure which a well-trained mind always ought to feel in recanting a fallacious doctrine. But you do me the justice to understand that of course I do not take this step I propose—for my personal satisfaction. No, sir, it is the value of my example to others, which purifies my motives and animates my soul."

After this concluding and noble sentence, the conversation drooped. Host and guest both felt they had had enough of each other. Kenelm soon rose to depart.

Mr. Roach, on taking leave of him at the door, said, with marked emphasis—

"Not for my personal satisfaction—remember that. Whenever you hear my conversion discussed in the world, say that from my own lips you heard these words—NOT FOR MY PERSONAL SATISFACTION. No! My kind regards to Welby—a married man himself, and a father; *he* will understand me."

CHAPTER IX.

On quitting Oxford, Kenelm wandered for several days about the country, advancing to no definite goal, meeting with no noticeable adventure. At last he found himself mechanically retracing his steps. A magnetic influence he could not resist drew him back towards the grassy meads and the sparkling rill of Moleswick.

"There must be," said he to himself, "a mental, like an optical, illusion. In the last, we fancy we have seen a spectre. If we dare not face the apparition—dare not attempt to touch it—run superstitiously away from it—what happens? We shall believe to our dying day that it was not an illusion—that it was a spectre—and so we may be crazed for life. But if we manfully walk up to the Phantom, stretch our hands to seize it, lo! it fades into thin air, the cheat of our eyesight is dispelled, and we shall never be ghost-ridden again. So it must be with this mental illusion of mine. I see an image strange to my experience—it seems to me, at that first sight, clothed with a supernatural charm; like an unreasoning coward, I run away from it. It continues to haunt me; I cannot shut out its apparition. It pursues me by day alike in the haunts of men—alike in the solitudes of nature; it visits me by night in my dreams. I begin to say this must be a real visitant from another world—it must be love—the love of which I read in the Poets, as in the Poets I read of witchcraft and ghosts. Surely I must approach that apparition as a philosopher like Sir David Brewster would approach the black cat seated on a hearthrug, which he tells us that some lady of his acquaintance constantly saw till she went into a world into which black cats are not held to be admitted. The more I think of it the less it appears to me possible that I can be really in love with a wild, half-educated, anomalous creature, merely because the apparition of her face haunts me. With perfect safety, therefore, I can approach that creature; in proportion as I see more of her, the illusion will vanish. I will go back to Moleswick manfully."

Thus said Kenelm to himself, and himself answered—

"Go; for thou canst not help it. Thinkest thou that Daces can escape the net that has meshed a Roach? No—

'Come it will, the day decreed by fate,'

when thou must succumb to the 'nature which will be heard.' Better succumb now, and with a good grace, than resist till thou hast reached thy fiftieth year, and then make a rational choice not for thy personal satisfaction."

Whereupon Kenelm answered to himself, indignantly, "Pooh! thou flippant. My *alter ego*, thou knowest not what thou art talking about! It is not a question of nature; it is a question of the supernatural—an illusion—a phantom!"

Thus Kenelm and himself continued to quarrel with each other; and the more they quarrelled, the nearer they approached to the haunted spot in which had been seen, and fled from, the fatal apparition of first love.

BOOK VI.

CHAPTER I.

Sir Peter had not heard from Kenelm since a letter informing him that his son had left town on an excursion, which would probably be short, though it might last a few weeks; and the good Baronet now resolved to go to London himself, take his chance of Kenelm's return, and if still absent, at least learn from Mivers and others how far that very eccentric planet had contrived to steer a regular course amidst the fixed stars of the metropolitan system. He had other reasons for his journey. He wished to make the acquaintance of Chillingly Gordon before handing him over the £20,000 which Kenelm had released in that resettlement of estates, the necessary deeds of which the young heir had signed before quitting London for Moleswick. Sir Peter wished still more to see Cecilia Travers, in whom Kenelm's accounts of her had inspired a very strong interest.

The day after his arrival in town Sir Peter breakfasted with Mivers.

"Upon my word you are very comfortable here," said Sir Peter, glancing at the well-appointed table, and round the well-furnished rooms.

"Naturally so—there is no one to prevent my being comfortable. I am not married:—taste that omelette."

"Some men declare they never knew comfort till they were married, cousin Mivers."

"Some men are reflecting bodies, and catch a pallid gleam from the comfort which a wife concentres on herself. With a fortune so modest and secure, what comforts, possessed by me now, would not a Mrs. Chillingly Mivers ravish from my hold and appropriate to herself! Instead of these pleasant rooms, where should I be lodged? In a dingy den looking on a backyard, excluded from the sun by day and vocal with cats by night; while Mrs. Mivers luxuriated in two drawing-rooms with southern aspect and perhaps a boudoir. My brougham would be torn from my uses and monopolized by 'the angel of my hearth,' clouded in her crinoline and halved by her chignon. No! if ever I marry—and I never deprive myself of the civilities and needlework which single ladies waste upon me, by saying I shall not marry—it will be when women have fully established their rights; for then, men may have a chance of vindicating their own. Then, if there are two drawing-rooms in the house, I shall take one, if not, we will toss up who shall have the back parlour; if we keep a brougham, it will be exclusively mine three days in the week; if Mrs. M. wants £200 a year for her wardrobe, she must be contented with one, the other half will belong to my personal decoration; if I am oppressed by proof sheets and printers' devils, half of the oppression falls to her lot, while I take my holiday on the croquet ground at Wimbledon. Yes, when the present wrongs of women are exchanged for equality with men—I will cheerfully marry; and to do the thing generous, I will not oppose Mrs.

M.'s voting in the vestry or for Parliament. I will give her my own votes with pleasure."

"I fear, my dear cousin, that you have infected Kenelm with your selfish ideas on the nuptial state. He does not seem inclined to marry—Eh?"

"Not that I know of."

"What sort of girl is Cecilia Travers?"

"One of those superior girls who are not likely to tower into that terrible giantess called 'a superior woman.' A handsome, well educated, sensible young lady. Not spoilt by being an heiress—in fine, just the sort of girl whom you could desire to fix on for a daughter-in-law."

"And you don't think Kenelm has a fancy for her?"

"Honestly speaking—I do not."

"Any counter-attraction? There are some things in which sons do not confide in their fathers. You have never heard that Kenelm has been a little wild?"

"Wild he is, as the noble savage who ran in woods," said cousin Mivers.

"You frighten me!"

"Before the noble savage ran across the squaws, and was wise enough to run away from them. Kenelm has run away now, somewhere."

"Yes, he does not tell me where, nor do they know at his lodgings. A heap of notes on his table and no directions where they are to be forwarded. On the whole, however, he has held his own in London society—Eh?"

"Certainly! he has been more courted than most young men, and perhaps more talked of. Oddities generally are."

"You own he has talents above the average? Do you not think he will make a figure in the world some day, and discharge that debt to the literary stores or the political interests of his country, which alas, I and my predecessors, the other Sir Peters, failed to do; and for which I hailed his birth and gave him the name of Kenelm?"

"Upon my word," answered Mivers—who had now finished his breakfast, retreated to an easy chair, and taken from the chimney-piece one of his famous trabucos,—"upon my word I can't guess; if some great reverse of fortune befell him, and he had to work for his livelihood, or if some other direful calamity gave a shock to his nervous system and jolted it into a fussy fidgety direction, I dare say he might make a splash in that current of life which bears men on to the grave. But you see he wants, as he himself very truly says, the two stimulants to definite action—poverty and vanity."

"Surely there have been great men who were neither poor nor vain?"

"I doubt it. But vanity is a ruling motive that takes many forms and many aliases—call it ambition, call it love of fame, still its substance is the same—the desire of applause carried into fussiness of action."

"There may be the desire for abstract truth without care for applause."

"Certainly. A philosopher on a desert island may amuse himself by meditating on the distinction between light and heat. But if on returning to the world, he publish the result of his meditations, vanity steps in, and desires to be applauded."

"Nonsense, cousin Mivers, he may rather desire to be of use and benefit to mankind. You don't deny that there is such a thing as philanthropy."

"I don't deny that there is such a thing as humbug. And whenever I meet a man who has the face to tell me, that he is taking a great deal of trouble, and putting himself very much out of his way, for a philanthropical object, without the slightest idea of reward either in praise or pence, I know that I have a humbug before me—a dangerous humbug—a swindling humbug—a fellow with his pocket full of villainous prospectuses and appeals to subscribers."

"Pooh, pooh; leave off that affectation of cynicism; you are not a bad-hearted fellow—you must love mankind—you must have an interest in the welfare of posterity."

"Love mankind? Interest in posterity? Bless my soul, Cousin Peter, I hope you have no prospectuses in *your* pockets; no schemes for draining the Pontine Marshes out of pure love to mankind; no propositions for doubling the income tax, as a reserve fund for posterity, should our coalfields fail three thousand years hence. Love of mankind! Rubbish! This comes of living in the country."

"But you do love the human race—you do care for the generations that are to come."

"I! Not a bit of it. On the contrary, I rather dislike the human race, taking it altogether, and including the Australian bushmen; and I don't believe any man who tells me that he would grieve half as much if ten millions of human beings were swallowed up by an earthquake at a considerable distance from his own residence, say Abyssinia, as he would for a rise in his butcher's bills. As to posterity, who would consent to have a month's fit of the gout or tic-douloureux in order that in the fourth thousand year, A. D., posterity should enjoy a perfect system of sewage?"

Sir Peter, who had recently been afflicted by a very sharp attack of neuralgia, shook his head, but was too conscientious not to keep silence.

"To turn the subject," said Mivers, relighting the cigar which he had laid aside while delivering himself of his amiable opinions, "I think you would do well, while in town, to call on your old friend Travers, and be introduced to Cecilia. If you think as favourably of her as I do, why not ask father and daughter to pay you a visit at Exmundham? Girls think more about a man when they see the place which he can offer to them as a home, and Exmundham is an attractive place to girls—picturesque and romantic."

"A very good idea," cried Sir Peter, heartily. "And I want also to make the acquaintance of Chillingly Gordon. Give me his address."

"Here is his card on the chimney-piece, take it; you will always find him at home till two o'clock. He is too sensible to waste the forenoon in riding out in Hyde Park with young ladies."

"Give me your frank opinion of that young

kinsman. Kenelm tells me that he is clever and ambitious."

"Kenelm speaks truly. He is not a man who will talk stuff about love of mankind and posterity. He is of our day, with large keen wide-awake eyes, that look only on such portions of mankind as can be of use to him—and do not spoil their sight by poring through cracked telescopes, to catch a glimpse of posterity. Gordon is a man to be a Chancellor of the Exchequer, perhaps a Prime Minister."

"And old Gordon's son is cleverer than my boy—than the namesake of Kenelm Digby!" and Sir Peter sighed.

"I did not say that. I am cleverer than Chillingly Gordon, and the proof of it is that I am too clever to wish to be Prime Minister—very disagreeable office—hard work—irregular hours for meals—much abuse and confirmed dyspepsia."

Sir Peter went away rather downhearted. He found Chillingly Gordon at home in a lodging in Jermyn Street. Though prepossessed against him by all he had heard, Sir Peter was soon propitiated in his favour. Gordon had a frank man-of-the-world way with him, and much too fine a tact to utter any sentiments likely to displease an old-fashioned country gentleman, and a relation who might possibly be of service in his career. He touched briefly, and with apparent feeling, on the unhappy litigation commenced by his father; spoke with affectionate praise of Kenelm; and with a discriminating good-nature of Mivers, as a man who, to parody the epigram on Charles II.

> "Never says a kindly thing
> And never does a harsh one."

Then he drew Sir Peter on to talk of the country and agricultural prospects. Learned that among his objects in visiting town, was the wish to inspect a patented hydraulic ram that might be very useful for his farmyard, which was ill supplied with water. Startled the Baronet by evincing some practical knowledge of mechanics; insisted on accompanying him to the city to inspect the ram; did so, and approved the purchase;

took him next to see a new American reaping-machine, and did not part with him till he had obtained Sir Peter's promise to dine with him at the Garrick; an invitation peculiarly agreeable to Sir Peter, who had a natural curiosity to see some of the more recently distinguished frequenters of that social club. As, on quitting Gordon, Sir Peter took his way to the house of Leopold Travers, his thoughts turned with much kindliness towards his young kinsman. "Mivers and Kenelm," quoth he to himself, "gave me an unfavourable impression of this lad; they represent him as worldly, self-seeking, and so forth. But Mivers takes such cynical views of character, and Kenelm is too eccentric to judge fairly of a sensible man of the world. At all events it is not like an egotist to put himself out of his way to be so civil to an old fellow like me. A young man about town must have pleasanter modes of passing his day than inspecting hydraulic rams and reaping-machines. Clever they allow him to be. Yes, decidedly clever—and not offensively clever—practical."

Sir Peter found Travers in the drawing-room with his daughter, Mrs. Campion, and Lady Glenalvon. Travers was one of those men rare in middle age, who are more often to be found in their drawing-room than in their private study; he was fond of female society; and perhaps it was this predilection which contributed to preserve in him the charm of good breeding and winning manners. The two men had not met for many years; not indeed since Travers was at the zenith of his career of fashion, and Sir Peter was one of those pleasant *dilettanti* and half humouristic conversationalists who become popular and courted diners-out.

Sir Peter had originally been a moderate Whig because his father had been one before him, but he left the Whig party with the Duke of Richmond, Mr. Stanley (afterwards Lord Derby), and others, when it seemed to him that that party had ceased to be moderate.

Leopold Travers had, as a youth in the Guards, been a high Tory, but, siding with Sir Robert Peel on the repeal of the Corn Laws, remained with the Peelites after the bulk of the Tory party had renounced the guidance of their former chief, and now went with these Peelites in whatever direction the progress of the age might impel their strides in advance of Whigs and in defiance of Tories.

However, it is not the politics of these two gentlemen that are in question now. As I have just said, they had not met for many years. Travers was very little changed. Sir Peter recognised him at a glance; Sir Peter was much changed, and Travers hesitated before, on hearing his name announced, he felt quite sure that it was the right Sir Peter towards whom he advanced, and to whom he extended his cordial hand. Travers preserved the colour of his hair and the neat proportions of his figure, and was as scrupulously well dressed as in his dandy days. Sir Peter, originally very thin and with fair locks and dreamy blue eyes, had now become rather portly, at least towards the middle of him—very grey—had long ago taken to spectacles—his dress too was very old fashioned, and made by a country tailor. He looked quite as much a gentleman as Travers did; quite perhaps as healthy, allowing for difference of years; quite as likely to last his time. But between them was the difference of the nervous temperament and the lymphatic. Travers, with less brain than Sir Peter, had kept his brain constantly active; Sir Peter had allowed his brain to dawdle over old books and lazy delight in letting the hours slip by. Therefore Travers still looked young—alert—up to his day, up to anything; while Sir Peter, entering that drawing-room, seemed a sort of Rip van Winkle who had slept through the past generation, and looked on the present with eyes yet drowsy. Still, in those rare moments when he was thoroughly roused up, there would have been found in Sir Peter a glow of heart, nay, even a vigour of thought, much more expressive than the constitutional alertness that characterized Leopold Travers, of the attributes we most love and admire in the young.

"My dear Sir Peter, is it you? I am so glad to see you again," said Travers. "What an age since we met, and how condescendingly kind you were then to me; silly fop that I was! But bygones are bygones; come to the present. Let me introduce to you, first, my valued friend, Mrs. Campion, whose distinguished husband you remember. Ah, what pleasant meetings we had at his house! And next, that young lady of whom she takes motherly charge; my daughter Cecilia. Lady Glenalvon, your wife's friend, of course needs no introduction, time stands still with her."

Sir Peter lowered his spectacles, which in reality he only wanted for books in small print, and gazed attentively on the three ladies—at each gaze a bow. But while his eyes were still lingeringly fixed on Cecilia, Lady Glenalvon advanced, naturally in right of rank and the claim of old acquaintance, the first of the three to greet him.

"Alas, my dear Sir Peter! time does not stand still for any of us; but what matter, if it leaves pleasant footprints! When I see you again, my youth comes before me. My early friend, Caroline Brotherton, now Lady Chillingly; our girlish walks with each other; wreaths and ball-dresses the practical topic; prospective husbands, the dream at a distance. Come and sit here: tell me all about Caroline."

Sir Peter, who had little to say about Caroline that could possibly interest anybody but himself, nevertheless took his seat beside Lady Glenalvon, and, as in duty bound, made the most flattering account of his She Baronet which experience or invention would allow. All the while, however, his thoughts were on Kenelm, and his eyes on Cecilia.

Cecilia resumes some mysterious piece of lady's work—no matter what—perhaps embroidery for a music-stool, perhaps a pair of slippers for her father (which, being rather vain of his feet and knowing they looked best in plain morocco, he will certainly never wear). Cecilia appears absorbed in her occupation; but her eyes and her thoughts are on Sir Peter. Why, my lady reader may guess. And oh, so flatteringly, so lovingly fixed! She thinks he has a most charming, intelligent, benignant countenance. She admires even his old-fashioned frock-coat, high neckcloth, and strapped trousers. She venerates his grey hairs, pure of dye. She tries to find a close resemblance between that fair, blue-eyed, plumpish, elderly gentleman and the lean, dark-eyed, saturnine, lofty Kenelm; she detects the likeness which nobody else would. She begins to love Sir Peter, though he has not said a word to her.

Ah! on this, a word for what it is worth to you, my young readers. You, sir, wishing to marry a girl who is to be deeply, lastingly in love with you, and a thoroughly good wife practically, consider well how she takes to your parents—how she attaches to them an inexpressible sentiment, a disinterested reverence—even should you but dimly recognize the sentiment, or feel the reverence, how if between you and your parents some little cause of coldness arise, she will charm you back to honour your father and your mother, even though they are not particularly genial to her—well, if you win that sort of girl as your wife, think you have got a treasure. You have won a woman to whom Heaven has given the two best attributes—intense feeling of love, intense sense of duty. What, my dear lady reader, I say of one sex, I say of another, though in a less degree; because a girl who marries becomes of her husband's family, and the man does not become of his wife's. Still I distrust the depth of any man's love to a woman, if he does not feel a great degree of tenderness (and forbearance where differences arise) for her parents. But the wife must not so put them in the foreground as to make the husband think he is cast into the cold of the shadow. Pardon this intolerable length of digression, dear reader—it is not altogether a digression, for it belongs to my tale that you should clearly understand the sort of girl that is personified in Cecilia Travers.

"What has become of Kenelm?" asks Lady Glenalvon.

"I wish I could tell you," answers Sir Peter. "He wrote me word that he was going forth on rambles into 'fresh woods and pastures new,' perhaps for some weeks. I have not had a word from him since."

"You make me uneasy," said Lady Glenalvon. "I hope nothing can have happened to him—he cannot have fallen ill."

Cecilia stops her work, and looks up wistfully.

"Make your mind easy," said Travers with a laugh; "I am in his secret. He has challenged the champion of England, and gone into the country to train."

"Very likely," said Sir Peter quietly; "I should not be in the least surprised, should you, Miss Travers?"

"I think it more probable that Mr. Chillingly is doing some kindness to others which he wishes to keep concealed."

Sir Peter was pleased with this reply, and drew his chair nearer to Cecilia's. Lady Glenalvon, charmed to bring those two together, soon rose and took leave.

Sir Peter remained nearly an hour talking chiefly with Cecilia, who won her way into his heart with extraordinary ease; and he did not quit the house till he had engaged her father, Mrs. Campion, and herself to pay him a week's visit at Exmundham, towards the end of the London season, which was fast approaching.

Having obtained this promise, Sir Peter went away, and ten minutes after Mr. Gordon Chillingly entered the drawing-room. He had already established a visiting acquaintance with the Traverses. Travers had taken a liking to him. Mrs. Campion found him an extremely well-informed, unaffected young man, very superior to young men in general. Cecilia was cordially polite to Kenelm's cousin.

Altogether that was a very happy day for Sir Peter. He enjoyed greatly his dinner at the Garrick, where he met some old acquaintances, and was presented to some new "celebrities." He observed that Gordon stood well with these eminent persons. Though as yet undistinguished himself, they treated him with a certain respect, as well as with evident liking. The most eminent of them, at least the one with the most solidly-established reputation, said in Sir Peter's ear, "You may be proud of your nephew, Gordon!"

"He is not my nephew, only the son of a very distant cousin."

"Sorry for that. But he will shed lustre on kinsfolk, however distant. Clever fellow, yet popular; rare combination—sure to rise."

Sir Peter suppressed a gulp in the throat. "Ah, if some one as eminent had spoken thus of Kenelm!"

But he was too generous to allow that half-envious sentiment to last more than a moment. Why should he not be proud of any member of the family who could irradiate the antique obscurity of the Chillingly race? And how agreeable this clever young man made himself to Sir Peter!

The next day Gordon insisted on accompanying him to see the latest acquisitions in the British Museum, and various other exhibitions, and went at night to the Prince of Wales's Theatre, where Sir Peter was infinitely delighted with an admirable little comedy by Mr. Robertson, admirably placed on the stage by Marie Wilton. The day after, when Gordon called on him at his hotel, he cleared his throat, and thus plunged at once into the communication he had hitherto delayed.

"Gordon, my boy, I owe you a debt, and I am now, thanks to Kenelm, able to pay it."

Gordon gave a little start of surprise, but remained silent.

"I told your father, shortly after Kenelm was born, that I meant to give up my London house, and lay by £1000 a year for you, in compensation for your chance of succeeding to Exmundham should I have died childless. Well, your father did not seem to think much of that promise, and went to law with me about certain unquestionable rights of mine. How so clever a man could have made such a mistake, would puzzle me, if I did not remember that he had a quarrelsome temper. Temper is a thing that often dominates cleverness—an uncontrollable thing; and allowances must be made for it. Not being of a quarrelsome temper myself (the Chillinglys are a placid race), I did not make the allowance for your father's differing, and (for a Chillingly) abnormal, constitution. The language and the tone of his letter respecting it, nettled me. I did not see why, thus treated, I should pinch myself to lay by a thousand a year. Facilities for buying a property most desirable for the possessor of Exmundham presented themselves. I bought it with borrowed money, and though I gave up the house in London, I did not lay by the thousand a year."

"My dear Sir Peter, I have always regretted that my poor father was misled—perhaps out of too paternal a care for my supposed interests—into that unhappy and fruitless litigation, after which no one could doubt that any generous intentions on your part would be finally abandoned. It has been a grateful surprise to me that I have been so kindly and cordially received into the family by Kenelm and yourself. Pray oblige me by dropping all reference to pecuniary matters—the idea of compensation to a very distant relative for the loss of expectations he had no right to form, is too absurd, for me at least, ever to entertain."

"But I am absurd enough to entertain it—though you express yourself in a very high-minded way. To come to the point, Kenelm is of age, and we have cut off the entail. The estate of course remains absolutely with Kenelm to dispose of, as it did before, and we must take it for granted that he will marry; at all events he cannot fall into your poor father's error; but whatever Kenelm hereafter does with his property, it is nothing to you, and is not to be counted upon. Even the title dies with Kenelm if he has no son. On resettling the estate, however, sums of money have been released which, as I stated before, enable me to discharge the debt which, Kenelm heartily agrees with me, is due to you. £20,000 are now lying at my bankers' to be transferred to yours; meanwhile, if you will call on my solicitor, Mr. Vining, Lincoln's-inn, you can see the new deed, and give to him your receipt for the £20,000 for which he holds my cheque. Stop—stop—stop—I will not hear a word—no thanks, they are not due."

Here Gordon, who had during this speech uttered various brief exclamations, which Sir Peter did not heed, caught hold of his kinsman's hand, and, despite of all struggles, pressed his lips on it. "I must thank you, I must give some vent to my emotions," cried Gordon. "This sum, great in itself, is far more to me than you can imagine—it opens my career—it assures my future."

"So Kenelm tells me; he said that sum would be more use to you now than ten times the amount twenty years hence."

"So it will—it will. And Kenelm consents to this sacrifice?"

"Consents—urges it!"

Gordon turned away his face, and Sir Peter resumed: "You want to get into Parliament; very natural ambition for a clever young fellow. I don't presume to dictate politics to you. I hear you are what is called a liberal; a man may be a liberal, I suppose, without being a Jacobin."

"I hope so, indeed. For my part I am anything but a violent man."

"Violent, no! Who ever heard of a violent Chillingly? But I was reading in the newspaper to-day a speech addressed to some populous audience, in which the orator was for dividing all the land and all the capital belonging to other people among the working class, calmly and quietly, without any violence, and deprecating violence; but saying, perhaps very truly, that the people to be robbed might not like it, and might offer violence; in which case woe betide them—it was they who would be guilty of violence—and they must take the consequences if they resisted the reasonable propositions of himself and his friends! That, I suppose, is among the new ideas with which Kenelm is more familiar than I am. Do you entertain those new ideas?"

"Certainly not—I despise the fools who do."

"And you will not abet revolutionary measures if you get into Parliament?"

"My dear Sir Peter—I fear you have heard very false reports of my opinions if you put such questions. "Listen," and therewith Gordon launched into dissertations very clever, very subtle, which committed him to nothing, beyond the wisdom of guiding popular opinion into right directions; what might be right directions he did not define, he left Sir Peter to guess them. Sir Peter did guess them, as Gordon meant he should, to be the directions which he, Sir Peter, thought right; and he was satisfied.

That subject disposed of, Gordon said, with much apparent feeling, "May I ask you to complete the favours you have lavished on me. I have never seen Exmundham, and the home of the race from which I sprang has a deep interest for me. Will you allow me to spend a few days with you, and under the shade of your own trees take lessons in political science from one who has evidently reflected on it profoundly?"

"Profoundly—no—a little—a little, as a mere bystander," said Sir Peter modestly, but much flattered. "Come, my dear boy, by all means; you will have a hearty welcome. By-the-by, Travers and his handsome daughter promise to visit me in about a fortnight, why not come at the same time?"

A sudden flash lit up the young man's countenance. "I shall be so delighted," he cried.

"I am but slightly acquainted with Mr. Travers, but I like him much, and Mrs. Campion is so well informed."

"And what say you to the girl?"

"The girl, Miss Travers. Oh, she is very well in her way. But I don't talk with young ladies more than I can help."

"Then you are like your cousin Kenelm?"

"I wish I were like him in other things."

"No, one such oddity in a family is quite enough. But though I would not have you change to a Kenelm, I would not change Kenelm for the most perfect model of a son that the world can exhibit." Delivering himself of this burst of parental fondness, Sir Peter shook hands with Gordon, and walked off to Mivers, who was to give him luncheon, and then accompany him to the station. Sir Peter was to return to Exmundham by the afternoon express.

Left alone, Gordon indulged in one of those luxurious guesses into the future which form the happiest moments in youth, when so ambitious as his. The sum Sir Peter placed at his disposal would ensure his entrance into Parliament. He counted with confidence on early successes there. He extended the scope of his views. With such successes he might calculate with certainty on a brilliant marriage, augmenting his fortune, and confirming his position. He had previously fixed his thoughts on Cecilia Travers—I will do him the justice to say not from mercenary motives alone, but not certainly with the impetuous ardour of youthful love. He thought her exactly fitted to be the wife of an eminent public man, in person, acquirement, dignified yet popular manners. He esteemed her, he liked her, and then her fortune would add solidity to his position. In fact, he had that sort of rational attachment to Cecilia which wise men, like Lord Bacon and Montaigne, would commend to another wise man seeking a wife. What opportunities of awaking in herself a similar, perhaps a warmer, attachment the visit to Exmundham would afford! He had learned when he had called on the Traverses that they were going thither, and hence that burst of family sentiment which had procured the invitation to himself.

But he must be cautious, he must not prematurely awaken Travers' suspicions. He was not as yet a match that the squire could approve of for his heiress. And, though he was ignorant of Sir Peter's designs on that young lady, he was much too prudent to confide his own to a kinsman, of whose discretion he had strong misgivings. It was enough for him at present that way was opened for his own resolute energies. And cheerfully, though musingly, he weighed its obstacles, and divined its goal, as he paced his floor with bended head and restless strides, now quick, now slow.

Sir Peter, in the meanwhile, found a very good luncheon prepared for him at Mivers's rooms, which he had all to himself, for his host never "spoilt his dinner and insulted his breakfast" by that intermediate meal. He remained at his desk writing brief notes of business, or of pleasure, while Sir Peter did justice to lamb cutlets and grilled chicken. But he looked up from his task, with raised eyebrows, when Sir Peter, after a somewhat discursive account of his visit to the Traverses, his admiration of Cecilia, and the adroitness with which, acting on his cousin's hint, he had engaged the family to spend a few days at Exmundham, added, "And by-the-by, I have asked young Gordon to meet them."

"To meet them; meet Mr. and Miss Travers! you have? I thought you wished Kenelm to marry Cecilia. I was mistaken, you meant Gordon!"

"Gordon," exclaimed Sir Peter, dropping his knife and fork. "Nonsense, you don't suppose that Miss Travers prefers him to Kenelm, or that he has the presumption to fancy that her father would sanction his addresses."

"I indulge in no suppositions of the sort. I content myself with thinking that Gordon is clever, insinuating, young; and it is a very good chance of bettering himself that you have thrown in his way. However, it is no affair of mine; and though on the whole I like Kenelm better than Gordon, still I like Gordon very well, and I have an interest in following his career which I can't say I have in conjecturing what may be Kenelm's—more likely no career at all."

"Mivers, you delight in provoking me; you do say such uncomfortable things. But, in the first place, Gordon spoke rather slightingly of Miss Travers."

"Ah, indeed; that's a bad sign," muttered Mivers.

Sir Peter did not hear him, and went on.

"And, besides, I feel pretty sure that the dear girl has already a regard for Kenelm which allows no room for a rival. However I shall not forget your hint, but keep a sharp look-out; and if I see the young man wants to be too sweet on Cecilia, I shall cut short his visit."

"Give yourself no trouble in the matter; it will do no good. Marriages are made in heaven. Heaven's will be done. If I can get away I will run down to you for a day or two. Perhaps in that case you can ask Lady Glenalvon. I like her, and she likes Kenelm. Have you finished? I see the brougham is at the door, and we have to call at your hotel to take up your carpet bag."

Mivers was deliberately sealing his notes while he thus spoke. He now rang for his servant, gave orders for their delivery, and then followed Sir Peter downstairs and into the brougham. Not a word would he say more about Gordon, and Sir Peter shrank from telling him about the £20,000. Chillingly Mivers was perhaps the last person to whom Sir Peter would be tempted to parade an act of generosity. Mivers might not unfrequently do a generous act himself, provided it was not divulged; but he had always a sneer for the generosity of others.

CHAPTER II.

WANDERING back towards Moleswick, Kenelm found himself a little before sunset on the banks of the garrulous brook, almost opposite to the house inhabited by Lily Mordaunt. He stood long and silently by the grassy margin, his dark shadow falling over the stream, broken into fragments by the eddy and strife of waves, fresh from their leap down the neighbouring waterfall. His eyes rested on the house and the garden lawn in the front. The upper windows were open. "I wonder which is hers," he said to himself. At last he caught a glimpse of the gardener, bending over a flower border with his watering-pot, and then moving slowly through the little shrubbery, no doubt to his own cottage. Now the lawn was solitary, save that a couple of thrushes dropped suddenly on the sward.

"Good evening, sir," said a voice. "A capital spot for trout this."

Kenelm turned his head, and beheld on the footpath, just behind him, a respectable elderly man, apparently of the class of a small retail tradesman, with a fishing-rod in his hand and a basket belted to his side.

"For trout," replied Kenelm; "I dare say. A strangely attractive spot indeed."

"Are you an angler, sir, if I may make bold to inquire?" asked the elderly man, somewhat perhaps puzzled as to the rank of the stranger; noticing, on the one hand, his dress and his mien, on the other, slung to his shoulders, the worn and shabby knapsack which Kenelm had carried, at home and abroad, the preceding year.

"Aye, I am an angler."

"Then this is the best place in the whole stream. Look, sir, there is Izaak Walton's summer-house; and further down you see that white, neat-looking house. Well, that is my house, sir, and I have an apartment which I let to gentlemen anglers. It is generally occupied throughout the summer months. I expect every day to have a letter to engage it, but it is vacant now. A very nice apartment, sir—sitting-room and bed-room."

"*Descende cœlo, et dic age tibia,*" said Kenelm.

"Sir!" said the elderly man.

"I beg you ten thousand pardons. I have had the misfortune to have been at the university, and to have learned a little Latin, which sometimes comes back very inopportunely. But, speaking in plain English, what I meant to say is this: I invoked the Muse to descend from heaven and bring with her—the original says a fife, but I meant—a fishing-rod. I should think your apartment would suit me exactly; pray show it to me."

"With the greatest pleasure," said the elderly man. "The Muse need not bring a fishing-rod! we have all sorts of tackle at your service, and a boat too, if you care for that. The stream hereabouts is so shallow and narrow that a boat is of little use till you get farther down."

"I don't want to get farther down; but should I want to get to the opposite bank, without wading across, would the boat take me, or is there a bridge?"

"The boat can take you. It is a flat-bottomed punt, and there is a bridge too for foot pas sengers, just opposite my house; and between this and Moleswick, where the stream widens, there is a ferry. The stone bridge for traffic is at the farther end of the town."

"Good. Let us go at once to your house."

The two men walked on.

"By-the-by," said Kenelm as they walked, "do you know much of the family who inhabit the pretty cottage on the opposite side, which we have just left behind?"

"Mrs. Cameron's. Yes, of course, a very good lady; and Mr. Melville, the painter. I am sure I ought to know, for he has often lodged with me when he came to visit Mrs. Cameron. He recommends my apartment to his friends, and they are my best lodgers. I like painters, sir, though I don't know much about paintings. They are pleasant gentlemen, and easily contented with my humble roof and fare."

"You are quite right. I don't know much about paintings myself, but I am inclined to believe that painters, judging not from what I have seen of them, for I have not a single acquaintance among them personally, but from what I have read of their lives, are, as a general rule, not only pleasant but noble gentlemen. They form within themselves desires to beautify or exalt commonplace things, and they can only accomplish their desires by a constant study of what is beautiful and what is exalted. A man constantly so engaged ought to be a very noble gentleman, even though he may be the son of a shoeblack. And living in a higher world than we do, I can conceive that he is, as you say, very well contented with humble roof and fare in the world we inhabit."

"Exactly, sir; I see—I see now, though you put it in a way that never struck me before."

"And yet," said Kenelm, looking benignly at the speaker, "you seem to me a well-educated and intelligent man; reflective on things in general, without being unmindful of your interests in particular, especially when you have lodgings to let. Do not be offended. That sort of man is not perhaps born to be a painter, but I respect him highly. The world, sir, requires the vast majority of its inhabitants to live in it—to live by it. 'Each for himself, and God for us all.' The greatest happiness of the greatest number is best secured by a prudent consideration for Number One."

Somewhat to Kenelm's surprise (allowing that he had now learned enough of life to be occasionally surprised) the elderly man here made a dead halt, stretched out his hand cordially, and cried, "Hear, hear! I see that, like me, you are a decided democrat."

"Democrat! Pray, may I ask, not why you are one—that would be a liberty, and democrats resent any liberty taken with themselves—but why you suppose I am?"

"You spoke of the greatest happiness of the greatest number. That is a democratic sentiment surely! Besides, did not you say, sir, that painters—painters, sir, painters, even if they were the sons of shoeblacks, were the true gentlemen—the true noblemen?"

"I did not say that exactly, to the disparagement of other gentlemen and nobles. But if I did, what then?"

"Sir, I agree with you. I despise rank, I despise dukes, and earls, and aristocrats. 'An honest man's the noblest work of God.' Some poet says that. I think Shakespeare. Wonderful man, Shakespeare. A tradesman's son—butcher, I believe. Eh! My uncle was a butcher, and might have been an alderman. I go along with you heartily, heartily. I am a democrat, every inch of me. Shake hands, sir—shake hands; we are all equals. 'Each for himself, and God for us all.'"

"I have no objection to shake hands," said Kenelm; "but don't let me owe your condescension to false pretences. Though we are all equal before the law, except the rich man, who has little chance of justice as against a poor man when submitted to an English jury, yet I utterly deny that any two men you select can be equals. One must beat the other in something, and when one man beats another, democracy ceases and aristocracy begins."

"Aristocracy! I don't see that. What do you mean by aristocracy?"

"The ascendency of the better man. In a rude State the better man is the stronger; in a corrupt State, perhaps the more roguish; in modern republics the jobbers get the money and the lawyers get the power. In well-ordered States alone aristocracy appears at its genuine worth: the better man in birth, because respect for ancestry secures a higher standard of honour; the better man in wealth, because of the immense uses to enterprise, energy, and the fine arts, which rich men must be if they follow their natural inclinations; the better man in character, the better man in ability, for reasons too obvious to define; and these two last will beat the others in the government of the State, if the State be flourishing and free. All these four classes of better men constitute true aristocracy; and when a better government than a true aristocracy shall be devised by the wit of man, we shall not be far off from the Millennium and the reign of saints. But here we are at the house—yours, is it not? I like the look of it extremely."

The elderly man now entered the little porch, over which clambered honeysuckle and ivy intertwined, and ushered Kenelm into a pleasant parlour, with a bay window, and an equally pleasant bedroom behind it.

"Will it do, sir?"

"Perfectly. I take it from this moment. My knapsack contains all I shall need for the night. There is a portmanteau of mine at Mr. Somers's shop, which can be sent here in the morning."

"But we have not settled about the terms," said the elderly man, beginning to feel rather doubtful whether he ought thus to have installed in his home a stalwart pedestrian of whom he knew nothing, and who, though talking glibly enough on other things, had preserved an ominous silence on the subject of payment.

"Terms—true, name them."

"Including board?"

"Certainly. Chameleons live on air, Democrats on wind-bags. I have a more vulgar appetite, and require mutton!"

"Meat is very dear now-a-days," said the elderly man, "and I am afraid, for board and lodging, I cannot charge you less than £3 3s.—say £3 a week. My lodgers usually pay a week in advance."

"Agreed," said Kenelm, extracting three sovereigns from his purse. "I have dined already—I want nothing more this evening; let me detain you no further. Be kind enough to shut the door after you."

When he was alone, Kenelm seated himself in the recess of the bay window, against the casement, and looked forth intently. Yes—he was right—he could see from thence the home of Lily. Not, indeed, more than a white gleam of the house through the interstices of trees and shrubs—but the gentle lawn sloping to the brook, with the great willow at the end dipping its boughs into the water, and shutting out all view beyond itself by its bower of tender leaves. The young man bent his face on his hands and mused dreamily: the evening deepened, the stars came forth, the rays of the moon now peered aslant through the arching dips of the willow, silvering their way as they stole to the waves below.

"Shall I bring lights, sir? or do you prefer a lamp or candles?" asked a voice behind; the voice of the elderly man's wife. "Do you like the shutters closed?"

The questions startled the dreamer. They seemed mocking his own old mockings on the romance of love. Lamp or candles, practical lights for prosaic eyes, and shutters closed against moon and stars!

"Thank you, ma'am, not yet," he said; and rising quietly he placed his hand on the window-sill, swung himself through the open casement, and passed slowly along the margin of the rivulet by a path chequered alternately with shade and starlight; the moon yet more slowly rising above the willows, and lengthening its track along the wavelets.

CHAPTER III.

THOUGH Kenelm did not think it necessary at present to report to his parents, or his London acquaintances, his recent movements and his present resting-place, it never entered into his head to lurk *perdu* in the immediate vicinity of Lily's house, and seek opportunities of meeting her clandestinely. He walked to Mrs. Braefield's he next morning, found her at home, and said in rather a more off-hand manner than was habitual to him, "I have hired a lodging in your neighbourhood, on the banks of the brook, for the sake of its trout-fishing. So you will allow me to call on you sometimes, and one of these days I hope you will give me the dinner that I so unceremoniously rejected some days ago. I was then summoned away suddenly, much against my will."

"Yes; my husband said that you shot off from him with a wild exclamation about duty."

"Quite true; my reason, and I may say my conscience, were greatly perplexed upon a matter extremely important and altogether new to me. I went to Oxford—the place above all others in which questions of reason and conscience are most deeply considered, and perhaps least satisfactorily solved. Relieved in my mind by my visit to a distinguished ornament of that university, I felt I might indulge in a summer holiday, and here I am."

"Ah! I understand. You had religious doubts—thought perhaps of turning Roman Catholic. I hope you are not going to do so?"

"My doubts were not necessarily of a religious nature. Pagans have entertained them."

"Whatever they were I am pleased to see they did not prevent your return," said Mrs. Braefield graciously. "But where have you found a lodging—why not have come to us? My husband would have been scarcely less glad than myself to receive you."

"You say that so sincerely, and so cordially, that to answer by a brief 'I thank you' seems rigid and heartless. But there are times in life when one yearns to be alone—to commune with one's own heart, and, if possible, be still; I am in one of those moody times. Bear with me."

Mrs. Braefield looked at him with affectionate, kindly interest. She had gone before him through the solitary load of young romance. She remembered her dreamy, dangerous girlhood, when she, too, had yearned to be alone.

"Bear with you—yes, indeed. I wish, Mr. Chillingly, that I were your sister, and that you would confide in me. Something troubles you."

"Troubles me—no. My thoughts are happy ones, and they may sometimes perplex me, but they do not trouble." Kenelm said this very softly; and in the warmer light of his musing eyes, the sweeter play of his tranquil smile, there was an expression which did not belie his words.

"You have not told me where you have found a lodging," said Mrs. Braefield, somewhat abruptly.

"Did I not!" replied Kenelm, with an unconscious start, as from an abstracted reverie. "With no undistinguished host, I presume, for when I asked him this morning for the right address of his cottage, in order to direct such luggage as I have to be sent there, he gave me his card with a grand air, saying, 'I am pretty well known at Moleswick, by and beyond it.' I have not yet looked at his card. Oh, here it is—'Algernon Sidney Gale Jones, Cromwell Lodge'—you laugh. What do you know of him?"

"I wish my husband were here; he would tell you more about him. Mr. Jones is quite a character."

"So I perceive."

"A great radical—very talkative and troublesome at the vestry; but our vicar, Mr. Emlyn, says there is no real harm in him—that his bark is worse than his bite—and that his republican or radical notions must be laid to the door of his godfathers! In addition to his name of Jones, he was unhappily christened Gale; Gale Jones being a noted radical orator at the time of his birth. And I suppose Algernon Sidney was prefixed to Gale in order to devote the new-born more emphatically to republican principles."

"Naturally, therefore, Algernon Sidney Gale Jones baptizes his house Cromwell Lodge, seeing that Algernon Sidney held the Protectorate in especial abhorrence, and that the original Gale Jones, if an honest radical, must have done the same, considering what rough usage the advocates of parliamentary reform met with at the hands of his Highness. But we must be indulgent to men who have been unfortunately christened before they had any choice of the names that were to rule their fate. I myself should have been less whimsical had I not been named after a Kenelm who believed in sympathetic powders. Apart from his political doctrines, I like my landlord—he keeps his wife in excellent order. She seems frightened at the sound of her own footsteps, and glides to and fro, a pallid image of submissive womanhood in list slippers."

"Great recommendations certainly, and Cromwell Lodge is very prettily situated. By-the-by, it is very near Mrs. Cameron's."

"Now I think of it, so it is," said Kenelm innocently.

Ah! my friend Kenelm, enemy of shams, and truthteller *par excellence*, what hast thou come to! How are the mighty fallen! "Since you say you will dine with us, suppose we fix the day after to-morrow, and I will ask Mrs. Cameron and Lily."

"The day after to-morrow—I shall be delighted."

"An early hour?"

"The earlier the better."

"Is six o'clock too early?"

"Too early—certainly not—on the contrary—— Good-day—I must now go to Mrs. Somers, she has charge of my portmanteau."

Then Kenelm rose.

"Poor dear Lily!" said Mrs. Braefield; "I wish she were less of a child."

Kenelm re-seated himself.

"Is she a child? I don't think she is actually a child."

"Not in years; she is between seventeen and eighteen; but my husband says that she is too childish to talk to, and always tells me to take her off his hands; he would rather talk with Mrs. Cameron."

"Indeed!"

"Still I find something in her."

"Indeed!"

"Not exactly childish, nor quite womanish."

"What then?"

"I can't exactly define. But you know what Mr. Melville and Mrs. Cameron call her, as a pet name?"

"No."

"Fairy! Fairies have no age; fairy is neither child nor woman."

"Fairy. She is called Fairy by those who know her best? Fairy!"

"And she believes in fairies."

"Does she?—so do I. Pardon me, I must be off. The day after to-morrow—six o'clock."

"Wait one moment," said Elsie, going to her writing-table. "Since you pass Grasmere on your way home, will you kindly leave this note?"

"I thought Grasmere was a lake in the north?"

"Yes; but Mr. Melville chose to call the cottage by the name of the lake. I think the first picture he ever sold was a view of Wordsworth's house there. Here is my note to ask Mrs. Cameron to meet you; but if you object to be my messenger——"

"Object! my dear Mrs. Braefield. As you say, I pass close by the cottage."

CHAPTER IV.

Kenelm went with somewhat rapid pace from Mrs. Braefield's to the shop in the High Street, kept by Will Somers. Jessie was behind the counter, which was thronged with customers. Kenelm gave her a brief direction about his portmanteau, and then passed into the back parlour where her husband was employed on his baskets —with the baby's cradle in the corner, and its grandmother rocking it mechanically, as she read a wonderful missionary tract full of tales of miraculous conversions: into what sort of Christians we will not pause to inquire.

"And so you are happy, Will?" said Kenelm, seating himself between the basket-maker and the infant; the dear old mother beside him, reading the tract which linked her dreams of life eternal with life just opening in the cradle that she rocked. He not happy! How he pitied the man who could ask such a question.

"Happy, sir! I should think so, indeed. There is not a night on which Jessie and I, and mother too, do not pray that some day or other you may be as happy. By-and-by the baby will learn to pray 'God bless papa, and mamma, grand-mamma, and Mr. Chillingly.'"

"There is some one else much more deserving of prayers than I, though needing them less. You will know some day—pass it by now. To return to the point; you are happy; if I asked why, would not you say, 'Because I have married the girl I love, and have never repented?'"

"Well, sir, that is about it; though begging your pardon, I think it could be put more prettily somehow."

"You are right there. But perhaps love and happiness never yet found any words that could fitly express them. Good-bye, for the present."

Ah! if it were as mere materialists, or as many middle-aged or elderly folks, who if materialists are so without knowing it, unreflectingly say, "The main element of happiness is bodily or animal health and strength," that question which Chillingly put would appear a very unmeaning or a very insulting one addressed to a pale cripple, who, however improved of late in health, would still be sickly and ailing all his life,—put, too, by a man of the rarest conformation of physical powers that nature can adapt to physical enjoyment—a man who, since the age in which memory commences, had never known what it was to be unwell, who could scarcely understand you if you talked of a finger-ache, and whom those refinements of mental culture which multiply the delights of the senses had endowed with the most exquisite conceptions of such happiness as mere nature and its instincts can give! But Will did not think the question unmeaning or insulting. He, the poor cripple, felt a vast superiority on the scale of joyous being over the young Hercules, well-born, cultured, and wealthy, who could know so little of happiness as to ask the crippled basket-maker if he were happy—he, blessed husband and father!

CHAPTER V.

Lily was seated on the grass under a chestnut-tree on the lawn. A white cat, not long emerged from kittenhood, curled itself by her side. On her lap was an open volume, which she was reading with the greatest delight.

Mrs. Cameron came from the house, looked round, perceived the girl, and approached; and either she moved so gently, or Lily was so absorbed in her book, that the latter was not aware of her presence till she felt a light hand on her shoulder, and, looking up, recognised her aunt's gentle face.

"Ah! Fairy, Fairy, that silly book when you ought to be at your French verbs. What will your guardian say when he comes and finds you have so wasted time?"

"He will say that fairies never waste their time; and he will scold you for saying so." Therewith Lily threw down the book, sprang up to her feet, wound her arm round Mrs. Cameron's neck, and kissed her fondly. "There! is *that* wasting time? I love you so, aunty. In a day like this I think I love everybody and everything!" As she said this, she drew up her lithe form, looked into the blue sky, and with parted lips seemed to drink in air and sunshine. Then she woke up the dozing cat, and began chasing it round the lawn.

Mrs. Cameron stood still, regarding her with moistened eyes. Just at that moment Kenelm entered through the garden gate. He, too, stood still, his eyes fixed on the undulating movements of Fairy's exquisite form. She had arrested her favourite, and was now at play with it, shaking off her straw hat, and drawing the ribbon attached to it tantalizingly along the smooth grass. Her rich hair thus released and dishevelled by the exercise, fell partly over her face in wavy ringlets; and her musical laugh and words of sportive endearment, sounded on Kenelm's ear more joyously than the trill of the sky-lark, more sweetly than the coo of the ring-dove.

He approached towards Mrs. Cameron. Lily turned suddenly and saw him. Instinctively she smoothed back her loosened tresses, replaced the straw hat, and came up demurely to his side just as he had accosted her aunt.

"Pardon my intrusion, Mrs. Cameron. I am the bearer of this note from Mrs. Braefield." While the aunt read the note, he turned to the niece.

"You promised to show me the picture, Miss Mordaunt."

"But that was a long time ago."

"Too long to expect a lady's promise to be kept?"

Lily seemed to ponder that question, and hesitated before she answered.

"I will show you the picture. I don't think I ever broke a promise yet, but I shall be more careful how I make one in future."

"Why so?"

"Because you did not value mine when I made it, and that hurt me." Lily lifted up her head with a bewitching stateliness, and added gravely, "I was offended."

"Mrs. Braefield is very kind," said Mrs. Cameron; "she asks us to dine the day after to-morrow. You would like to go, Lily?"

"All grown-up people, I suppose? No, thank you, dear aunt. You go alone, I would rather stay at home. May I have little Clemmy to play with! She will bring Juba, and Blanche is very partial to Juba, though she does scratch him."

"Very well, my dear, you shall have your playmate, and I will go by myself."

Kenelm stood aghast. "You will not go, Miss Mordaunt; Mrs. Braefield will be so disappointed. And if you don't go, whom shall I have to talk to? I don't like grown-up people better than you do."

"You are going?"

"Certainly."

"And if I go you will talk to me? I am afraid of Mr. Braefield. He is so wise."

"I will save you from him, and will not utter a grain of wisdom."

"Aunty, I will go."

Here Lily made a bound and caught up Blanche, who, taking her kisses resignedly, stared with evident curiosity upon Kenelm.

Here a bell within the house rung the announcement of luncheon. Mrs. Cameron invited Kenelm to partake of that meal. He felt as Romulus might have felt when first invited to taste the ambrosia of the gods. Yet certainly that luncheon was not such as might have pleased Kenelm Chillingly in the early days of The Temperance Hotel. But somehow or other of late he had lost appetite; and on this occasion a very modest share of a very slender dish of chicken fricasseed, and a few cherries daintily arranged on vine leaves, which Lily selected for him, contented him—as probably a very little ambrosia contented Romulus while feasting his eyes on Hebe.

Luncheon over, while Mrs. Cameron wrote her reply to Elsie, Kenelm was conducted by

Lily into her own *own* room, in vulgar parlance her *boudoir*, though it did not look as if any one ever *bouder*'d there. It was exquisitely pretty—pretty not as a woman's, but a child's dream of the own own room she would like to have—wondrously neat and cool, and pure-looking; a trellis paper, the trellis gay with roses and woodbine, and birds and butterflies; draperies of muslin, festooned with dainty tassels and ribbons; a dwarf bookcase, that seemed well stored, at least as to bindings; a dainty little writing-table in French *marqueterie*—looking too fresh and spotless to have known hard service. The casement was open, and in keeping with the trellis paper; woodbine and roses from without encroached on the window-sides, gently stirred by the faint summer breeze, and wafting sweet odours into the little room. Kenelm went to the window, and glanced on the view beyond. "I was right," he said to himself; "I divined it." But though he spoke in a low inward whisper, Lily, who had watched his movements in surprise, overheard.

"You divined it. Divined what?"

"Nothing, nothing; I was but talking to myself."

"Tell me what you divined—I insist upon it!" and Fairy petulantly stamped her tiny foot on the floor.

"Do you? Then I obey. I have taken a lodging for a short time on the other side of the brook—Cromwell Lodge—and seeing your house as I passed, I divined that your room was in this part of it. How soft here is the view of the water! Ah! yonder is Izaak Walton's summer-house."

"Don't talk about Izaak Walton or I shall quarrel with you, as I did with Lion when he wanted me to like that cruel book."

"Who is Lion?"

"Lion—of course, my guardian. I called him Lion when I was a little child. It was on seeing in one of his books a print of a lion playing with a little child."

"Ah! I know the design well," said Kenelm, with a slight sigh. "It is from an antique Greek gem. It is not the lion that plays with the child, it is the child that masters the lion, and the Greeks called the child 'Love.'"

This idea seemed beyond Lily's perfect comprehension. She paused before she answered, with the *naïveté* of a child six years old—

"I see now why I mastered Blanche, who will not make friends with any one else—I love Blanche. Ah, that reminds me—come and look at the picture."

She went to the wall over the writing-table, drew a silk curtain aside from a small painting in a dainty velvet framework, and pointing to it, cried with triumph—"Look there! is it not beautiful?"

Kenelm had been prepared to see a landscape, or a group, or anything but what he did see—it was the portrait of Blanche when a kitten.

Little elevated though the subject was, it was treated with graceful fancy. The kitten had evidently ceased from playing with the cotton reel that lay between her paws, and was fixing her gaze intent on a bullfinch that had lighted on a spray within her reach.

"You understand," said Lily, placing her hand on his arm and drawing him towards what she thought the best light fot the picture; "It is Blanche's first sight of a bird. Look well at her face; don't you see a sudden surprise—half joy, half fear? She ceases to play with the reel. Her intellect—or, as Mr. Braefield would say, 'her instinct'—is for the first time aroused. From that moment Blanche was no longer a mere kitten. And it required, oh, the most careful education, to teach her not to kill the poor little birds. She never does now, but I had such trouble with her."

"I cannot say honestly that I do see all that you do in the picture; but it seems to me very simply painted, and was, no doubt, a striking likeness of Blanche at that early age."

"So it was. Lion drew the first sketch from life with his pencil; and when he saw how pleased I was with it—he was so good—he put it on canvas, and let me sit by him while he painted it. Then he took it away, and brought it back finished and framed as you see, last May, a present for my birthday."

"You were born in May — with the flowers."

"The best of all the flowers are born before May—violets."

"But they are born in the shade, and cling to it. Surely, as a child of May, you love the sun!"

"I love the sun — it is never too bright nor too warm for me. But I don't think that, though born in May, I was born in sunlight. I feel more like my own native self when I creep into she shade and sit down alone. I can weep then."

As she thus shyly ended, the character of her whole countenance was changed—its infantine mirthfulness was gone; a grave, thoughtful, even a sad, expression settled on the tender eyes and the tremulous lips.

Kenelm was so touched that words failed him,

and there was silence for some moments between the two. At length Kenelm said slowly—

"You say your own native self. Do you then, feel, as I often do, that there is a second, possibly a *native*, self, deep hid beneath the self—not merely what we show to the world in common (that may be merely a mask)—but the self that we ordinarily accept even when in solitude as our own; an inner innermost self; oh, so different and so rarely coming forth from its hiding-place; asserting its right of sovereignty, and putting out the other self, as the sun puts out a star?"

Had Kenelm thus spoken to a clever man of the world—to a Chillingly Mivers—to a Chillingly Gordon—they certainly would not have understood him. But to such men he never would have thus spoken. He had a vague hope that this childlike girl, despite so much of childlike talk, would understand him; and she did, at once.

Advancing close to him, again laying her hand on his arm, and looking up towards his bended face with startled wondering eyes, no longer sad, yet not mirthful—

"How true! You have felt that too? Where *is* that innermost self, so deep down—so deep; yet when it does come forth, so much higher—higher—immeasurably higher than one's everyday self? It does not tame the butterflies—it longs to get to the stars. And then—and then—ah, how soon it fades back again! You have felt that. Does it not puzzle you?"

"Very much."

"Are there no wise books about it that help to explain?"

"No wise books in my very limited reading even hint at the puzzle. I fancy that it is one of those insoluble questions that rest between the infant and his Maker. Mind and soul are not the same things, and what you and I call 'wise men' are always confounding the two——"

Fortunately for all parties—especially the reader; for Kenelm had here got on the back of one of his most cherished hobbies—the distinction between psychology and metaphysics — soul and mind scientifically or logically considered—Mrs. Cameron here entered the room and asked him how he liked the picture.

"Very much. I am no great judge of the art. But it pleased me at once, and now that Miss Mordaunt has interpreted the intention of the painter, I admire it yet more."

"Lily chooses to interpret his intention in her own way, and insists that Blanche's expression of countenance conveys an idea of her capacity to restrain her destructive instinct, and be taught to believe that it is wrong to kill birds for mere sport. For food she need not kill them, seeing that Lily takes care that she has plenty to eat. But I don't think that Mr. Melville had the slightest suspicion that he had indicated that capacity in his picture."

"He must have done so, whether he suspected it or not," said Lily positively; "otherwise he would not be truthful."

"Why not truthful?" asked Kenelm.

"Don't you see? If you were called upon

to describe truthfully the character of any little child, would you only speak of such naughty impulses as all children have in common, and not even hint at the capacity to be made better?"

"Admirably put!" said Kenelm. "There is no doubt that a much fiercer animal than a cat —a tiger, for instance, or a conquering hero—may be taught to live on the kindest possible terms with the creatures on which it was its natural instinct to prey."

"Yes—yes; hear that, aunty! You remember the Happy Family that we saw, eight years ago, at Moleswick Fair, with a cat not half so nice as Blanche allowing a mouse to bite her ear? Well then would Lion not have been shamefully false to Blanche if Lion had not——"

Lily paused and looked half shyly, half archly, at Kenelm, then added, in slow, deep-drawn tones—"given a glimpse of her innermost self?"

"Innermost self!" repeated Mrs. Cameron, perplexed, and laughing gently.

Lily stole nearer to Kenelm and whispered—

"Is not one's innermost self one's best self?"

Kenelm smiled approvingly. The fairy was rapidly deepening her spell upon him. If Lily had been his sister, his betrothed, his wife, how fondly he would have kissed her! She had expressed a thought over which he had often inaudibly brooded, and she had clothed it with all the charm of her own infantine fancy and womanlike tenderness! Goethe has said somewhere, or is reported to have said, "There is something in every man's heart, that, if you knew it, would make you hate him." What Goethe said, still more what Goethe is reported to have said, is never to be taken quite literally. No comprehensive genius—genius at once poet and thinker—ever can be so taken. The sun shines on a dunghill. But the sun has no predilection for a dunghill. It only comprehends a dunghill as it does a rose. Still Kenelm had always regarded that loose ray from Goethe's prodigal orb with an abhorrence most unphilosophical for a philosopher so young as generally to take upon oath any words of so great a master. Kenelm thought that the root of all private benevolence, of all enlightened advance in social reform, lay in the adverse theorem—that in every man's nature there lies a something that, could we get at it, cleanse it, polish it, render it visibly clear to our eyes, would make us love him. And in this spontaneous, uncultured sympathy with the result of so many laborious struggles of his own scholastic intellect against the dogma of the German giant, he felt as if he had found a younger—true, but oh, how much more subduing, because so much younger—sister of his own man's soul.

Then came, so strongly, the sense of her sympathy with his own strange innermost self which a man will never feel more than once in his life with a daughter of Eve, that he dared not trust himself to speak. He somewhat hurried his leave-taking.

Passing in the rear of the garden towards the bridge which led to his lodging, he found on the opposite bank, at the other end of the bridge, Mr. Algernon Sidney Gale Jones, peacefully angling for trout.

"Will you not try the stream to-day, sir? Take my rod."

Kenelm remembered that Lily had called Izaak Walton's book "a cruel one," and shaking his head gently, went his way into the house. There he seated himself silently by the window, and looked towards the grassy lawn and the dipping willows, and the gleam of the white walls through the girdling trees, as he had looked the eve before.

"Ah!" he murmured at last, "if, as I hold, a man but tolerably good does good unconsciously merely by the act of living—if he can no more traverse his way from the cradle to the grave, without letting fall, as he passes, the germs of strength, fertility, and beauty, than can a reckless wind or a vagrant bird, which, where it passes, leaves behind it the oak, the cornsheaf, or the flower—ah, if that be so, how tenfold the good must be, if the man find the gentler and purer duplicate of his own being in that mysterious, undefinable union which Skakespeares and day-labourers equally agree to call love; which Newton never recognises, and which Descartes (his only rival in the realms of thought at once severe and imaginative) reduces into links of early association, explaining that he loved women who squinted because, when he was a boy, a girl with that infirmity squinted at him from the other side of his father's garden-wall! Ah! be this union between man and woman what it may; if it be really love—really the bond which embraces the innermost and bettermost self of both—how, daily, hourly, momently, should we bless God for having made it so easy to be happy and to be good!"

CHAPTER VI.

The dinner-party at Mr. Braefield's was not quite so small as Kenelm had anticipated. When the merchant heard from his wife that Kenelm was coming, he thought it would be but civil to the young gentleman to invite a few other persons to meet him.

"You see, my dear," he said to Elsie, "Mrs. Cameron is a very good, simple sort of woman, but not particularly amusing; and Lily, though a pretty girl, is so exceedingly childish. We owe much, my sweet Elsie, to this Mr. Chillingly"—here there was a deep tone of feeling in his voice and look—"and we must make it as pleasant for him as we can. I will bring down my friend Sir Thomas, and you ask Mr. Emlyn and his wife. Sir Thomas is a very sensible man, and Emlyn a very learned one. So Mr. Chillingly will find people worth talking to. By-the-by, when I go to town I will send down a haunch of venison from Groves'."

So when Kenelm arrived, a little before six o'clock, he found in the drawing-room the Rev. Charles Emlyn, vicar of Moleswick Proper, with his spouse, and a portly middle-aged man, to whom, as Sir Thomas Pratt, Kenelm was introduced. Sir Thomas was an eminent city banker. The ceremonies of introduction over, Kenelm stole to Elsie's side.

"I thought I was to meet Mrs. Cameron. I don't see her."

"She will be here presently. It looks as if it might rain, and I have sent the carriage for her and Lily. Ah, here they are!"

Mrs. Cameron entered, clothed in black silk. She always wore black; and behind her came Lily, in the spotless colour that became her name; no ornament, save a slender gold chain to which was appended a simple locket, and a single blush rose in her hair. She looked wonderfully lovely; and with that loveliness there was a certain nameless air of distinction, possibly owing to delicacy of form and colouring; possibly to a certain grace of carriage, which was not without a something of pride.

Mr. Braefield, who was a very punctual man, made a sign to his servant, and in another moment or so dinner was announced. Sir Thomas, of course, took in the hostess; Mr. Braefield, the vicar's wife (she was a dean's daughter); Kenelm, Mrs. Cameron; and the vicar, Lily.

On seating themselves at the table Kenelm was on the left-hand, next to the hostess, and separated from Lily by Mrs. Cameron and Mr. Emlyn; and when the vicar had said grace, Lily glanced behind his back and her aunt's at Kenelm (who did the same thing) making at him what the French call a *moue*. The pledge to her had been broken. She was between two men very much grown up—the vicar and the host. Kenelm returned the *moue* with a mournful smile and an involuntary shrug.

All were silent till, after his soup and his first glass of sherry, Sir Thomas began—

"I think, Mr. Chillingly, we have met before,

though I had not the honour then of making your acquaintance." Sir Thomas paused before he added, "Not long ago; the last State ball at Buckingham Palace."

Kenelm bent his head acquiescingly. He had been at that ball.

"You were talking with a very charming woman—a friend of mine—Lady Glenalvon."

(Sir Thomas was Lady Glenalvon's banker.)

"I remember perfectly," said Kenelm. "We were seated in the picture gallery. You came to speak to Lady Glenalvon, and I yielded to you my place on the settee."

"Quite true; and I think you joined a young lady—very handsome—the great heiress, Miss Travers."

Kenelm again bowed, and turning away as politely as he could, addressed himself to Mrs. Cameron. Sir Thomas, satisfied that he had impressed on his audience the facts of his friendship with Lady Glenalvon and his attendance at the court ball, now directed his conversational powers towards the vicar, who, utterly foiled in the attempt to draw out Lily, met the baronet's advances with the ardour of a talker too long suppressed. Kenelm continued, unmolested, to ripen his acquaintance with Mrs. Cameron. She did not, however, seem to lend a very attentive ear to his preliminary commonplace remarks about scenery or weather, but at his first pause said,

"Sir Thomas spoke about a Miss Travers: is she related to a gentleman who was once in the Guards—Leopold Travers?"

"She is his daughter. Did you ever know Leopold Travers?"

"I have heard him mentioned by friends of mine long ago—long ago," replied Mrs. Cameron with a sort of weary languor, not unwonted, in her voice and manner; and then, as if dismissing the bygone reminiscence from her thoughts, changed the subject.

"Lily tells me, Mr. Chillingly, that you said you were staying at Mr. Jones's, Cromwell Lodge. I hope you are made comfortable there."

"Very. The situation is singularly pleasant."

"Yes, it is considered the prettiest spot on the brookside, and used to be a favourite resort for anglers; but the trout, I believe, are grown scarce; at least, now that the fishing in the Thames is improved, poor Mr. Jones complains that his old lodgers desert him. Of course you took the rooms for the sake of the fishing. I hope the sport may be better than it is said to be."

"It is of little consequence to me; I do not care much about fishing; and since Miss Mordaunt calls the book which first enticed me to take to it 'a cruel one,' I feel as if the trout had become as sacred as crocodiles were to the ancient Egyptians."

"Lily is a foolish child on such matters. She cannot bear the thought of giving pain to any dumb creature; and just before our garden there are a few trout which she has tamed. They feed out of her hand; she is always afraid they will wander away and get caught."

"But Mr. Melville is an angler?"

"Several years ago he would sometimes

pretend to fish, but I believe it was rather an excuse for lying on the grass and reading 'the cruel book,' or perhaps, rather, for sketching. But now he is seldom here till autumn, when it grows too cold for such amusement."

Here Sir Thomas's voice was so loudly raised that it stopped the conversation between Kenelm and Mrs. Cameron. He had got into some question of politics on which he and the vicar did not agree, and the discussion threatened to become warm, when Mrs. Braefield, with a woman's true tact, broached a new topic, in which Sir Thomas was immediately interested, relating to the construction of a conservatory for orchids that he meditated adding to his country-house, and in which frequent appeal was made to Mrs. Cameron, who was considered an accomplished florist, and who seemed at some time or other in her life to have acquired a very intimate acquaintance with the costly family of orchids.

When the ladies retired Kenelm found himself seated next to Mr. Emlyn, who astounded him by a complimentary quotation from one of his own Latin prize poems at the university, hoped he would make some stay at Moleswick, told him of the principal places in the neighbourhood worth visiting, and offered him the run of his library, which he flattered himself was rather rich, both in the best editions of Greek and Latin classics and in early English literature. Kenelm was much pleased with the scholarly vicar, especially when Mr. Emlyn began to speak about Mrs. Cameron and Lily. Of the first he said, "She is one of those women in whom Quiet is so predominant that it is long before one can know what under-currents of good feeling flow beneath the unruffled surface. I wish, however, she was a little more active in the management and education of her niece—a girl in whom I feel a very anxious interest, and whom I doubt if Mrs. Cameron understands. Perhaps, however, only a poet, and a very peculiar sort of poet, can understand her: Lily Mordaunt is herself a poem."

"I like your definition of her," said Kenelm.

"There is certainly something about her which differs much from the prose of common life."

"You probably know Wordsworth's lines:

'. . . and she shall lean her ear
In many a secret place
Where rivulets dance their wayward round,
And beauty, born of murmuring sound,
Shall pass into her face.'

They are lines that many critics have found unintelligible; but Lily seems like the living key to them."

Kenelm's dark face lighted up, but he made no answer.

"Only," continued Mr. Emlyn, "how a girl of that sort, left wholly to herself, untrained, undisciplined, is to grow up into the practical uses of womanhood, is a question that perplexes and saddens me."

"Any more wine?" asked the host, closing a conversation on commercial matters with Sir Thomas. "No?—shall we join the ladies?"

CHAPTER VII.

THE drawing-room was deserted; the ladies were in the garden. As Kenelm and Mr. Emlyn walked side by side towards the group (Sir Thomas and Mr. Braefield following at a little distance), the former asked, somewhat abruptly, "What sort of man is Miss Cameron's guardian, Mr. Melville?"

"I can scarcely answer that question. I see little of him when he comes here. Formerly, he used to run down pretty often with a harum-scarum set of young fellows, quartered at Cromwell Lodge—Grasmere had no accommodation for them—students in the Academy, I suppose. For some years he has not brought those persons, and when he does come himself it is but for a few days. He has the reputation of being very wild."

Further conversation was here stopped. The

two men, while they thus talked, had been diverging from the straight way across the lawn towards the ladies, turning into sequestered paths, through the shrubbery; now they emerged into the open sward, just before a table, on which coffee was served, and round which all the rest of the party were gathered.

"I hope, Mr. Emlyn," said Elsie's cheery voice, "that you have dissuaded Mr. Chillingly from turning papist. I am sure you have taken time enough to do so."

Mr. Emlyn, protestant every inch of him, slightly recoiled from Kenelm's side. "Do you meditate turning——" He could not conclude the sentence.

"Be not alarmed, my dear sir. I did but own to Mrs. Braefield that I had paid a visit to Oxford in order to confer with a learned man on a question that puzzled me, and as abstract as that feminine pastime, theology, is now-a-days. I cannot convince Mrs. Braefield that Oxford admits other puzzles in life than those which amuse the ladies." Here Kenelm dropped into a chair by the side of Lily.

Lily half-turned her back to him.

"Have I offended again?"

Lily shrugged her shoulders slightly and would not answer.

"I suspect, Miss Mordaunt, that among your good qualities, nature has omitted one; the better-most self within you should replace it."

Lily here abruptly turned to him her front face—the light of the skies was becoming dim, but the evening star shone upon it.

"How! what do you mean?"

"Am I to answer politely or truthfully?"

"Truthfully! Oh, truthfully! What is life without truth?"

"Even though one believes in fairies?"

"Fairies are truthful, in a certain way. But you are not truthful. You were not thinking of fairies when you—"

"When I what?"

"Found fault with me!"

"I am not sure of that. But I will translate

to you my thoughts, so far as I can read them myself, and to do so I will resort to the fairies. Let us suppose that a fairy has placed her changeling into the cradle of a mortal; that into the cradle she drops all manner of fairy gifts, which are not bestowed on mere mortals; but that one mortal attribute she forgets. The changeling grows up, she charms those around her; they humour, and pet, and spoil her. But there arises a moment in which the omission of the one mortal gift is felt by her admirers and friends. Guess what that is."

Lily pondered. "I see what you mean; the reverse of truthfulness, politeness."

"No, not exactly that, though politeness slides into it unawares; it is a very humble quality, a very unpoetic quality; a quality that many dull people possess; and yet without it no fairy can fascinate mortals, when on the face of the fairy settles the first wrinkle. Can you not guess it now?"

"No; you vex me, you provoke me;" and Lily stamped her foot petulantly, as in Kenelm's presence she had stamped it once before. "Speak plainly, I insist."

"Miss Mordaunt, excuse me, I dare not," said Kenelm, rising with the sort of bow one makes to the Queen; and he crossed over to Mrs. Braefield.

Lily remained, still pouting fiercely.

Sir Thomas took the chair Kenelm had vacated.

CHAPTER VIII.

The hour for parting came. Of all the guests, Sir Thomas alone staid at the house a guest for the night. Mr. and Mrs. Emlyn had their own carriage. Mrs. Braefield's carriage came to the door for Mrs. Cameron and Lily.

Said Lily, impatiently and discourteously, "Who would not rather walk on such a night?" and she whispered to her aunt.

Mrs. Cameron, listening to the whisper, and obedient to every whim of Lily's, said, "You are too considerate, dear Mrs. Braefield, Lily prefers walking home; there is no chance of rain now."

Kenelm followed the steps of the aunt and niece, and soon overtook them on the brookside.

"A charming night, Mr. Chillingly," said Mrs. Cameron.

"An English summer night; nothing like it in such parts of the world as I have visited. But, alas! of English summer nights there are but few."

"You have travelled much abroad?"

"Much—no, a little; chiefly on foot."

Lily hitherto had not said a word, and had been walking with downcast head. Now she looked up and said, in the mildest and most conciliatory of human voices—

"You have been abroad," then, with an acquiescence in the manners of the world which to him she had never yet manifested, she added his name, "Mr. Chillingly," and went on, more familiarly. "What a breadth of meaning the word 'abroad' conveys! Away, afar from oneself, from one's every-day life. How I envy you! you have been abroad: so has Lion"—(Here drawing herself up)—"I mean my guardian, Mr. Melville."

"Certainly, I have been abroad; but afar from myself—never. It is an old saying—all old sayings are true, most new sayings are false—a man carries his native soil at the sole of his foot."

Here the path somewhat narrowed. Mrs. Cameron went on first, Kenelm and Lily behind;

she, of course, on the dry path, he on the dewy grass.

She stopped him. "You are walking in the wet, and with those thin shoes." Lily moved instinctively away from the dry path.

Homely though that speech of Lily's be, and absurd as said by a fragile girl to a gladiator like Kenelm, it lit up a whole world of womanhood —it showed all that undiscoverable land which was hidden to the learned Mr. Emlyn, all that land which an uncomprehended girl seizes and reigns over when she becomes wife and mother.

At that homely speech, and that impulsive movement, Kenelm halted, in a sort of dreaming maze. He turned timidly—"Can you forgive me for my rude words? I presumed to find fault with you."

"And so justly. I have been thinking over all you said, and I feel you were so right; only I still do not quite understand what you meant by the quality for mortals which the fairy did not give to her changeling."

"If I did not dare say it before, I should still less dare to say it now."

"Do." There was no longer the stamp of the foot, no longer the flash from her eyes, no longer the wilfulness which said "I insist;"—"Do," soothingly, sweetly, imploringly.

Thus pushed to it, Kenelm plucked up courage, and not trusting himself to look at Lily, answered brusquely:

"The quality desirable for men, but more essential to women in proportion as they are fairy-like, though the tritest thing possible, is good temper."

Lily made a sudden bound from his side, and joined her aunt, walking through the wet grass.

When they reached the garden-gate Kenelm advanced and opened it. Lily passed him by haughtily; they gained the cottage-door.

"I don't ask you in at this hour," said Mrs. Cameron. "It would be but a false compliment."

Kenelm bowed and retreated. Lily left her aunt's side, and came towards him, extending her hand.

"I shall consider your words, Mr. Chillingly," she said, with a strangely majestic air. "At present I think you are not right. I am not ill-tempered; but"—here she paused, and then added with a loftiness of mien which, had she not been so exquisitely pretty, would have been rudeness —"in any case I forgive you."

CHAPTER IX.

THERE were a good many pretty villas in the outskirts of Moleswick, and the owners of them were generally well off, and yet there was little of what is called visiting society—owing, perhaps, to the fact that there not being among these proprietors any persons belonging to what is commonly called "the aristocratic class," there was a vast deal of aristocratic pretension. The family of Mr. A——, who had enriched himself as a stock-jobber, turned up its nose at the family of Mr. B——, who had enriched himself still more as a linendraper, while the family of Mr. B—— showed a very cold shoulder to the family of Mr. C——, who had become richer than either of them as a pawnbroker, and whose wife wore diamonds, but dropped her h's. England would be a community so aristocratic that there would be no living in it, if one could exterminate what is now called "aristocracy." The Braefields were the only persons who really drew together the antagonistic atoms of the Moleswick society, partly because they were acknowledged to be the first persons there, in right not only of old settlement (the Braefields had held Braefieldville for four generations), but of the wealth derived from those departments of commercial enterprise which are recognised as the highest, and of an establishment considered to be the most elegant in the neighbourhood; principally because Elsie, while exceedingly genial and cheerful in temper, had a certain power of will (as her runaway folly had manifested), and when she got people together compelled them to be civil to each other. She had commenced this gracious career by inaugurating children's parties, and when the children became friends the parents necessarily grew closer together. Still her task had only recently begun, and its effects were not in full operation. Thus, though it became known at Moleswick that a young gentleman, the heir to a baronetcy and a high estate, was sojourning at Cromwell Lodge, no overtures were made to him on the part of the A's, B's, and C's. The vicar, who called on Kenelm the day after the dinner at Braefieldville, explained to him the social conditions of the place. "You understand," said he, "that it will be from no want of courtesy on the part of my neighbours if they do not offer you any relief from the pleasures of solitude. It will be simply because they are shy, not because they are uncivil. And it is this consideration that makes me, at the risk of seeming too forward, entreat you to look into the vicarage any morning or evening on which you feel tired of your own company—suppose you drink tea with us this evening—you will find a young lady whose heart you have already won."

"Whose heart I have won!" faltered Kenelm, and the warm blood rushed to his cheek.

"But," continued the vicar, smiling, "she has no matrimonial designs on you at present. She is only twelve years old—my little girl Clemmy."

"Clemmy!—She is your daughter. I did

not know that. I very gratefully accept your invitation."

"I must not keep you longer from your amusement. The sky is just clouded enough for sport. What fly do you use?"

"To say truth, I doubt if the stream has much to tempt me in the way of its trout, and I prefer rambling about the lanes and by-paths to

'The noiseless angler's solitary stand.'

I am an indefatigable walker, and the home scenery round the place has many charms for me. Besides," added Kenelm, feeling conscious that he ought to find some more plausible excuse than the charms of home scenery for locating himself long in Cromwell Lodge—"besides—I intend to devote myself a good deal to reading. I have been very idle of late, and the solitude of this place must be favourable to study."

"You are not intended, I presume, for any of the learned professions?"

"The learned professions," replied Kenelm,

"is an invidious form of speech that we are doing our best to eradicate from the language. All professions now-a-days are to have much about the same amount of learning. The learning of the military profession is to be levelled upwards —the learning of the scholastic to be levelled downwards. Cabinet ministers sneer at the uses of Greek and Latin. And even such masculine studies as Law and Medicine are to be adapted to the measurements of taste and propriety in colleges for young ladies. No, I am not intended for any profession; but still an ignorant man like myself may not be the worse for a little book-reading now and then."

"You seem to be badly provided with books here," said the vicar, glancing round the room, in which, on a table in the corner, lay half-a-dozen old-looking volumes, evidently belonging not to the lodger but the landlord. "But, as I before said, my library is at your service. What branch of reading do you prefer?"

Kenelm was, and looked, puzzled. But after a pause he answered:

"The more remote it be from the present day, the better for me. You said your collection was rich in mediæval literature. But the Middle Ages are so copied by the modern Goths, that I might as well read translations of Chaucer, or take lodgings in Wardour Street. If you have any books about the manners and habits of those who, according to the newest idea in science, were our semi-human progenitors in the transition state between a marine animal and a gorilla, I should be very much edified by the loan."

"Alas," said Mr. Emlyn, laughing, "no such books have been left to us."

"No such books? You must be mistaken. There must be plenty of them somewhere. I grant all the wonderful powers of invention bestowed on the creators of poetic romance; still not the sovereign masters in that realm of literature—not Scott, not Cervantes, not Goethe, not even Shakespeare—could have presumed to rebuild the past without such materials as they found in the books that record it. And though I, no less cheerfully, grant that we have now living among us a creator of poetic romance immeasurably more inventive than they—appealing to our credulity in portents the most monstrous, with a charm of style the most conversationally familiar—still I cannot conceive that even that unrivalled romance-writer can so bewitch our understandings as to make us believe, that, if Miss Mordaunt's cat dislikes to wet her feet, it is probably because in the pre-historic age her ancestors lived in the dry country of Egypt; or that when some lofty orator, a Pitt or a Gladstone, rebuts with a polished smile which reveals his canine teeth the rude assault of an opponent, he betrays his descent from a "semi-human progenitor" who was accustomed to snap at his enemy. Surely—surely there must be some books still extant written by philosophers before the birth of Adam, in which there is authority, even though but in mythic fable, for such poetic inventions. Surely—surely some early chroniclers must depose that they saw, saw with their own eyes, the great gorillas who scratched off their hairy coverings to please the eyes of the young ladies of their species, and that they noted the gradual metamorphosis of one animal into another. For, if you tell me that this illustrious romance-writer is but a cautious man of science, and that we must accept his inventions according to the sober laws of evidence and fact, there is not the most incredible ghost story which does not better satisfy the common sense of a sceptic. However, if you have no such books, lend me the most unphilosophical you possess—on magic, for instance—the philosopher's stone——"

"I have some of them," said the vicar, laughing, "you shall choose for yourself."

"If you are going homeward, let me accompany you part of the way—I don't yet know where the church and the vicarage are, and I ought to know before I come in the evening."

Kenelm and the vicar walked side by side, very sociably, across the bridge and on the side of the rivulet on which stood Mrs. Cameron's cottage. As they skirted the garden pale at the rear of the cottage, Kenelm suddenly stopped in the middle of some sentence which had interested Mr. Emlyn, and as suddenly arrested his steps on the turf that bordered the lane. A little before him stood an old peasant woman, with whom Lily, on the opposite side of the garden pale, was conversing. Mr. Emlyn did not at first see what Kenelm saw; turning round rather to gaze on his companion, surprised by his abrupt halt and silence. The girl put a small basket into the old woman's hand, who then dropped a low curtsey, and uttered low a "God bless you." Low though it was, Kenelm overheard it, and said abstractedly to Mr. Emlyn, "Is there a greater link between this life and the next than God's blessing on the young, breathed from the lips of the old?"

CHAPTER X.

"AND how is your good man, Mrs. Haley?" said the vicar, who had now reached the spot on which the old woman stood—with Lily's fair face still bended down to her—while Kenelm slowly followed him.

"Thank you kindly, sir, he is better—out of his bed now. The young lady has done him a power of good——"

"Hush!" said Lily, colouring. "Make haste home now; you must not keep him waiting for his dinner."

The old woman again curtseyed, and went off at a brisk pace.

"Do you know, Mr. Chillingly," said Mr. Emlyn, "that Miss Mordaunt is the best doctor in the place? Though if she goes on making so many cures she will find the number of her patients rather burthensome."

"It was only the other day," said Lily, "that you scolded me for the best cure I have yet made."

"I?—Oh! I remember; you led that silly child Madge to believe that there was a fairy charm in the arrowroot you sent her. Own you deserved a scolding there."

"No, I did not. I dress the arrowroot, and am I not Fairy? I have just got such a pretty note from Clemmy, Mr. Emlyn, asking me to come up this evening and see her new magic-lantern. Will you tell her to expect me? And—mind—no scolding."

"And all magic?" said Mr. Emlyn; "be it so."

Lily and Kenelm had not hitherto exchanged a word. She had replied with a grave inclination of her head to his silent bow. But now she turned to him shyly and said, "I suppose you have been fishing all the morning?"

"No; the fishes hereabout are under the protection of a Fairy—whom I dare not displease."

Lily's face brightened, and she extended her

hand to him over the palings. "Good day; I hear aunty's voice—those dreadful French verbs!"

She disappeared among the shrubs, amid which they heard the trill of her fresh young voice singing to herself.

"That child has a heart of gold," said Mr. Emlyn, as the two men walked on. "I did not exaggerate when I said she was the best doctor in the place. I believe the poor really do believe that she is a Fairy. Of course we send from the vicarage to our ailing parishioners who require it food and wine; but it never seems to do them the good that her little dishes made by her own tiny hands do; and I don't know if you noticed the basket that old woman took away—Miss Lily taught Will Gower to make the prettiest little baskets; and she puts her jellies or other savories into dainty porcelain gallipots nicely fitting into the baskets, which she trims with ribbons. It is the look of the thing that tempts the appetite of the invalids, and certainly the child may well be called Fairy at present;

but I wish Miss Cameron would attend a little more strictly to her education. She can't be a Fairy for ever."

Kenelm sighed, but made no answer.

Mr. Emlyn then turned the conversation to erudite subjects, and so they came in sight of the town, when the vicar stopped and pointed towards the church, of which the spire rose a little to the left, with two aged yew-trees half shadowing the burial-ground, and in the rear a glimpse of the vicarage seen amid the shrubs of its garden ground.

"You will know your way now," said the vicar; "excuse me if I quit you, I have a few visits to make; among others, to poor Haley, husband to the old woman you saw. I read to him a chapter in the Bible every day; yet still I fancy that he believes in fairy charms."

"Better believe too much, than too little," said Kenelm; and he turned aside into the village, and spent half-an-hour with Will, looking at the pretty baskets Lily had taught Will to make.

Then, as he went slowly homeward, he turned aside into the churchyard.

The church, built in the thirteenth century, was not large, but it probably sufficed for its congregation, since it betrayed no signs of modern addition; restoration or repair it needed not. The centuries had but mellowed the tints of its solid walls, as little injured by the huge ivy stems that shot forth their aspiring leaves to the very summit of the stately tower, as by the slender roses which had been trained to climb up a foot or so of the massive buttresses. The site of the burial-ground was unusually picturesque: sheltered towards the north by a rising ground clothed with woods, sloping down at the south towards the glebe pasture grounds through which ran the brooklet, sufficiently near for its brawling gurgle to be heard on a still day. Kenelm sat himself on an antique tomb, which was evidently appropriated to some one of higher than common rank in bygone days, but on which the sculpture was wholly obliterated.

The stillness and solitude of the place had

their charm for his meditative temperament; and he remained there long, forgetful of time, and scarcely hearing the boom of the clock that warned him of its lapse.

When suddenly, a shadow—the shadow of a human form—fell on the grass on which his eyes dreamily rested. He looked up with a start, and beheld Lily standing before him mute and still. Her image was so present in his thoughts at the moment that he felt a thrill of awe, as if the thoughts had conjured up her apparition. She was the first to speak.

"You here, too?" she said very softly, almost whisperingly.

"Too!" echoed Kenelm, rising; "too! 'Tis no wonder that I, a stranger to the place, should find my steps attracted towards its most venerable building. Even the most careless traveller, halting at some remote abodes of the living, turns aside to gaze on the burial-ground of the dead. But my surprise is that you, Miss Mordaunt, should be attracted towards the same spot."

"It is my favourite spot," said Lily, "and

always has been. I have sat many an hour on that tombstone. It is strange to think that no one knows who sleeps beneath it. The 'Guide Book to Moleswick,' though it gives the history of the church from the reign in which it was first built, can only venture a guess that this tomb, the grandest and oldest in the burial-ground, is tenanted by some member of a family named Montfichet, that was once very powerful in the county, and has become extinct since the reign of Henry the Sixth. But," added Lily, "there is not a letter of the name Montfichet left. I found out more than any one else has done— I learned black-letter on purpose; look here," and she pointed to a small spot in which the moss had been removed. "Do you see those figures, are they not XVIII? and look again, in what was once the line above the figures, ELE. It must have been an Eleanor, who died at the age of eighteen——"

"I rather think it more probable that the figures refer to the date of the death, 1318 perhaps; and so far as I can decipher black-letter, which is more in my father's line than mine, I think it is A L, not E L, and that it seems as if there had been a letter between L and the second E, which is now effaced. The tomb itself is not likely to belong to any powerful family then resident at the place. Their monuments, according to usage, would have been within the church; probably in their own mortuary chapel."

"Don't try to destroy my fancy," said Lily, shaking her head; "you cannot succeed, I know *her* history too well. She was young, and some one loved her, and built over her the finest tomb he could afford; and see how long the epitaph must have been! how much it must have spoken in her praise, and of his grief. And then he went his way, and the tomb was neglected, and her fate forgotten."

"My dear Miss Mordaunt, this is indeed a wild romance to spin out of so slender a thread. But even if true, there is no reason to think that a life is forgotten though a tomb be neglected."

"Perhaps not," said Lily thoughtfully. "But

when I am dead, if I can look down, I think it would please me to see my grave not neglected by those who had loved me once."

She moved from him as she said this, and went to a little mound that seemed not long since raised; there was a simple cross at the head and a narrow border of flowers round it. Lily knelt beside the flowers and pulled out a stray weed. Then she rose, and said to Kenelm who had followed, and now stood beside her:

"She was the little grandchild of poor old Mrs. Hales. I could not cure her though I tried hard; she was so fond of me, and died in my arms. No; let me not say 'died,' surely there is no such thing as dying. 'Tis but a change of life:

"'Less than the void between two waves of air,
The space between existence and a soul.'"

"Whose lines are those?" asked Kenelm.

"I don't know; I learnt them from Lion. Don't you believe them to be true?"

"Yes! But the truth does not render the thought of quitting this scene of life for another more pleasing to most of us. See how soft and gentle and bright is all that living summer land beyond; let us find subject for talk from that, not from the graveyard on which we stand."

"But is there not a summer land fairer than that we see now; and which we do see, as in a dream, best when we take subjects of talk from the graveyard?" Without waiting for a reply Lily went on: "I planted these flowers; Mr. Emlyn was angry with me, he said it was 'popish.' But he had not the heart to have them taken up; I come here very often to see to them. Do you think it wrong? Poor little Nell!—she was so fond of flowers. And the Eleanor in the great tomb, she too perhaps knew some one who called her Nell; but there are no flowers round her tomb —Poor Eleanor."

She took the nosegay she wore on her bosom, and as she repassed the tomb laid it on the mouldering stone.

CHAPTER XI.

THEY quitted the burial ground, taking their way to Grasmere. Kenelm walked by Lily's side; not a word passed between them till they came in sight of the cottage.

Then Lily stopped abruptly, and lifting towards him her charming face, said:

"I told you I would think over what you said to me last night. I have done so, and feel I can thank you honestly. You were very kind; I never before thought that I had a bad temper, no one ever told me so. But I see now what you mean—sometimes I feel very quickly, and then I show it. But how did I show it to you, Mr. Chillingly?"

"Did you not turn your back to me when I seated myself next you in Mrs. Braefield's garden, vouchsafing me no reply when I asked if I had offended?"

Lily's face became bathed in blushes, and her voice faltered, as she answered.

"I was not offended, I was not in a bad temper then, it was worse than that."

"Worse—what could it possibly be?"

"I am afraid it was envy."

"Envy of what—of whom?"

"I don't know how to explain; after all I fear aunty is right, and the fairy tales put very silly, very naughty, thoughts into one's head. When Cinderella's sisters went to the king's ball, and Cinderella was left alone, did not she long to go too? Did not she envy her sisters?"

"Ah! I understand now—Sir Charles spoke of the Court Ball."

"And you were there talking with handsome ladies—and—Oh! I was so foolish and felt sore."

"You, who when we first met wondered how people who could live in the country preferred to live in towns, do then sometimes contradict yourself, and sigh for the great world that lies beyond these quiet water banks. You feel that you have youth and beauty, and wish to be admired!"

"It is not that exactly," said Lily, with a perplexed look in her ingenuous countenance, "and in my better moments, when the 'bettermost self' comes forth, I know that I am not made for the great world you speak of. But you see—" here she paused again, and as they had now entered the garden dropped wearily on a bench beside the path. Kenelm seated himself there too, waiting for her to finish her broken sentence.

"You see," she continued, looking down embarrassed, and describing vague circles on the gravel with her fairy-like foot, "that at home, ever since I can remember, they have treated me as if, well as if I were—what shall I say? the child of one of your great ladies. Even Lion, who is so noble, so grand, seemed to think when I was a mere infant that I was a little queen; once when I told a fib he did not scold me, but I never saw him look so sad and so angry as when he said, 'never again forget that you are a lady.' And, but I tire you——"

"Tire me, indeed! go on."

"No, I have said enough to explain why I have at times proud thoughts, and vain thoughts; and why for instance I said to myself: 'Perhaps my place of right is among those fine ladies whom he'—but it is all over now." She rose hastily with a pretty laugh, and bounded towards Mrs. Cameron, who was walking slowly along the lawn with a book in her hand.

CHAPTER XII.

It was a very merry party at the vicarage that evening. Lily had not been prepared to meet Kenelm there, and her face brightened wonderfully as at her entrance he turned from the book-shelves to which Mr. Emlyn was directing his attention. But instead of meeting his advance she darted off to the lawn, where Clemmy and several other children greeted her with a joyous shout.

"Not acquainted with Macleane's 'Juvenal'?" said the reverend scholar; "you will be greatly pleased with it—here it is—a posthumous work, edited by George Long. I can lend you Munro's Lucretius, '69. Aha! we have some scholars yet to pit against the Germans."

"I am heartily glad to hear it," said Kenelm. "It will be a long time before they will ever wish to rival us in that game which Miss Clemmy is now forming on the lawn, and in which England has recently acquired an European reputation."

"I don't take you. What game?"

"Puss in the Corner. With your leave I will look out and see whether it be a winning game for puss—in the long run." Kenelm joined the children, amidst whom Lily seemed not the least childlike. Resisting all overtures from Clemmy to join in their play, he seated himself on a sloping bank at a little distance—an idle looker on. His eye followed Lily's nimble movements, his ear drank in the music of her joyous laugh. Could that be the same girl whom he had seen tending the flower bed amid the gravestones! Mrs. Emlyn came across the lawn and joined him, seating herself also on the bank. Mrs. Emlyn was an exceedingly clever woman; nevertheless she was not formidable, on the contrary pleasing; and though the ladies in the neighbourhood said 'she talked like a book,' the easy gentleness of her voice carried off that offence.

"I suppose, Mr. Chillingly," said she, "I ought to apologize for my husband's invitation to what must seem to you so frivolous an entertainment as a child's party. But when Mr. Emlyn asked you to come to us this evening, he was not aware that Clemmy had also invited her young friends. He had looked forward to a rational conversation with you on his own favourite studies."

"It is not so long since I left school, but that I prefer a half holiday to lessons, even from a tutor so pleasant as Mr. Emlyn—

'Ah, happy years—once more who would not be a boy!' "

"Nay," said Mrs. Emlyn with a grave smile. "Who that had started so fairly as Mr. Chillingly in the career of man would wish to go back and resume a place among boys?"

"But, my dear Mrs. Emlyn, the line I quoted was wrung from the heart of a man who had already outstripped all rivals in the raceground he had chosen, and who at that moment was in the very Maytime of youth and of fame. And if such a man at such an epoch in his career could sigh to 'be once more a boy,' it must have bene when he was thinking of the boy's half holiday, and recoiling from the taskwork he was condemned to learn as man."

"The line you quote is, I think, from Childe Harold, and surely you would not apply to mankind in general the sentiment of a poet so peculiarly self-reflecting (if I may use that expression), and in whom sentiment is often so morbid."

"You are right Mrs. Emlyn," said Kenelm ingenuously. "Still a boy's half holiday is a very happy thing; and among mankind in general, there must be many who would be glad to have it back again. Mr. Emlyn himself, I should think."

"Mr. Emlyn has his half holiday now. Do you not see him standing just outside the window? Do you not hear him laughing? He is a child again in the mirth of his children. I hope you will stay some time in the neighbourhood, I am sure you and he will like each other. And it is such a rare delight to him to get a scholar like yourself to talk to."

"Pardon me, I am not a scholar—a very noble title that, and not to be given to a lazy trifler on the surface of book-lore like myself."

"You are too modest. My husband has a copy of your Cambridge prize verses, and says 'the Latinity of them is quite beautiful.' I quote his very words."

"Latin verse making is a mere knack, little more than a proof that one had an elegant scholar for one's tutor, as I certainly had. But it is by special grace that a real scholar can send forth another real scholar, and a Kennedy produce a Munro. But to return to the more interesting question of half holidays; I declare that Clemmy is leading off your husband in triumph. He is actually going to be Puss in the Corner."

"When you know more of Charles—I mean my husband—you will discover that his whole life is more or less of a holiday. Perhaps because he is not what you accuse yourself of being—he is not lazy; he never wishes to be a boy once more; and taskwork itself is holiday to him. He enjoys shutting himself up in his study and reading—he enjoys a walk with the children—he enjoys visiting the poor—he enjoys his duties as a clergyman. And though I am not always contented for him, though I think he should have had those honours in his profession which have been lavished on men with less ability and less learning, yet he is never discontented himself. Shall I tell you his secret?"

"Do."

"He is a *Thanks-giving Man*. You, too, must have much to thank God for, Mr. Chillingly; and in thanksgiving to God does there not blend usefulness to man, and such sense of pastime in the usefulness as makes each day a holiday?"

Kenelm looked up into the quiet face of this obscure pastor's wife with a startled expression in his own.

"I see, ma'am," said he, "that you have devoted much thought to the study of the æsthetical philosophy as expounded by German thinkers, whom it is rather difficult to understand."

"I, Mr. Chillingly—good gracious. No! What do you mean by your æsthetical philosophy?"

"According to æsthetics, I believe man arrives at his highest state of moral excellence when labour and duty lose all the harshness of effort —when they become the impulse and habit of life; when, as the essential attributes of the beautiful, they are, like beauty, enjoyed as pleasure; and thus, as you expressed, each day becomes a holiday. A lovely doctrine, not perhaps so lofty as that of the Stoics, but more bewitching. Only, very few of us can practically merge our cares and our worries into so serene an atmosphere."

"Some do so without knowing anything of æsthetics and with no pretence to be Stoics; but, then, they are Christians."

"There are some such Christians, no doubt, but they are rarely to be met with. Take Christendom altogether, and it appears to comprise the most agitated population in the world; the population in which there is the greatest grumbling as to the quantity of labour to be done, the loudest complaints that duty instead of a pleasure is a very hard and disagreeable struggle, and in which holidays are fewest and the moral atmosphere least serene. Perhaps," added Kenelm, with a deeper shade of thought on his brow, "it is this perpetual consciousness of struggle; this difficulty in merging toil into ease, or stern duty into placid enjoyment; this refusal to ascend for one's self into the calm of an air aloof from the cloud which darkens, and the hailstorm which beats upon, the fellow men we leave below; that makes the troubled life of Christendom nearer to heaven, and more conducive to heaven's design in rendering earth the wrestling ground and not the resting place of man, than is that of the Brahmin, ever seeking to abstract himself from the Christian's conflicts of action and desire, and to carry into its extremest practice the æsthetic theory, of basking undisturbed in the contemplation of the most absolute beauty human thought can reflect from its idea of divine good!"

Whatever Mrs. Emlyn might have said in reply was interrupted by the rush of the children towards her; they were tired of play, and eager for tea and the magic lantern.

CHAPTER XIII.

THE room is duly obscured and the white sheet attached to the wall; the children are seated, hushed, and awe-stricken. And Kenelm is placed next to Lily.

The tritest things in our mortal experience are among the most mysterious. There is more mystery in the growth of a blade of grass than there is in the wizard's mirror or the feats of a spirit medium. Most of us have known the attraction that draws one human being to another, and makes it so exquisite a happiness to sit quiet and mute by another's side; which stills for the moment the busiest thoughts in our brain, the most turbulent desires in our heart, and renders us but conscious of a present ineffable bliss. Most of us have known that. But who has ever been satisfied with any metaphysical account of its why or wherefore? We can but say it is love, and love at that earlier section of its history which has not yet escaped from romance: but by what process that other person has become singled out of the whole universe to attain such special power over one, is a problem that, though many have attempted to solve it, has never attained to solution. In the dim light of the room Kenelm could only distinguish the outlines of Lily's delicate face, but at each new surprise in the show, the face intuitively turned to his, and once, when the terrible image of a sheeted ghost, pursuing a guilty man, passed along the wall, she drew closer to him in her childish fright, and by an involuntary innocent movement laid her hand on his. He detained it tenderly, but, alas! it was withdrawn the next moment; the ghost was succeeded by a couple of dancing dogs. And Lily's ready laugh—partly at the dogs, partly at her own previous alarm—vexed Kenelm's ear. He wished there had been a succession of ghosts, each more appalling than the last.

The entertainment was over, and after a slight refreshment of cakes and wine-and-water the party broke up; the children-visitors went away attended by servant-maids who had come for them. Mrs. Cameron and Lily were to walk home on foot.

"It is a lovely night, Mrs. Cameron," said Mr. Emlyn, "and I will attend you to your gate."

"Permit me also," said Kenelm.

"Ay," said the vicar, "it is your own way to Cromwell Lodge."

The path led them through the churchyard as the nearest approach to the brookside. The moonbeams shimmered through the yew-trees and rested on the old tomb—playing, as it were, round the flowers which Lily's hand had, that day, dropped upon its stone. She was walking beside Kenelm—the elder two a few paces in front.

"How silly I was," said she, "to be so frightened at the false ghost! I don't think a real one would frighten me, at least if seen here, in this loving moonlight, and on God's ground!"

"Ghosts, were they permitted to appear except in a magic lantern, could not harm the innocent. And I wonder why the idea of their apparition should always have been associated with such phantasies of horror, especially by sinless children, who have the least reason to dread them."

"Oh, that is true," cried Lily; "but even when we are grown up there must be times in which we should so long to see a ghost, and feel what a comfort, what a joy it would be."

"I understand you. If some one very dear to us had vanished from our life; if we felt the anguish of the separation so intensely as to efface the thought that life, as you said so well, 'never dies;' well, yes, then I can conceive that the mourner would yearn to have a glimpse of the vanished one, were it but to ask the sole and only question he could desire to put: 'Art thou happy? May I hope that we shall meet again, never to part—never?'"

Kenelm's voice trembled as he spoke, tears stood in his eyes. A melancholy, vague, unaccountable, overpowering, passed across his heart, as the shadow of some dark-winged bird passes over a quiet stream.

"You have never yet felt this?" asked Lily

doubtingly, in a soft voice, full of tender pity, stopping short and looking into his face.

"I? No. I have never yet lost one whom I so loved and so yearned to see again. I was but thinking that such losses may befall us all ere we too vanish out of sight."

"Lily!" called forth Mrs. Cameron, halting at the gate of the burial-ground.

"Yes, auntie?"

"Mr. Emlyn wants to know how far you have got in 'Numa Pompilius.' Come and answer for yourself."

"Oh, those tiresome grown-up people!" whispered Lily, petulantly, to Kenelm. "I do like Mr. Emlyn; he is one of the very best of men. But still he is grown up, and his 'Numa Pompilius' is so stupid."

"My first French lesson-book. No, it is not stupid. Read on. It has hints of the prettiest fairy tale I know, and of the fairy in especial who bewitched my fancies as a boy."

By this time they had gained the gate of the burial-ground.

"What fairy tale? what fairy?" asked Lily, speaking quickly.

"She was a fairy, though in heathen language she is called a nymph—Egeria. She was the link between men and gods to him she loved; she belongs to the race of gods. True; she, too, may vanish, but she can never die."

"Well, Miss Lily," said the vicar, "and how far in the book I lent you—'Numa Pompilius'?"

"Ask me this day next week."

"I will; but mind you are to translate as you go on. I must see the translation."

"Very well. I will do my best," answered Lily meekly.

Lily now walked by the vicar's side, and Kenelm by Mrs. Cameron's, till they reached Grasmere.

"I will go on with you to the bridge, Mr. Chillingly," said the vicar, when the ladies had disappeared within their garden.

"We had little time to look over my books, and, by-the-by, I hope you at least took the 'Juvenal.'"

"No, Mr. Emlyn; who can quit your house with an inclination for satire? I must come some morning and select a volume from those works which give pleasant views of life and bequeath favourable impressions of mankind. Your wife, with whom I have had an interesting conversation upon the principles of æsthetical philosophy——"

"My wife—Charlotte! She knows nothing about æsthetical philosophy."

"She calls it by another name, but she understands it well enough to illustrate the principles by example. She tells me that labour and duty are so taken up by you

'In den heitern Regionen
Wo die reinen Formen wohnen,'

that they become joy and beauty—is it so?"

"I am sure that Charlotte never said any thing half so poetical. But, in plain words, the days pass with me very happily. I should be ungrateful if I were not happy. Heaven has bestowed on me so many sources of love—wife, children, books, and the calling which, when one quits one's own threshold, carries love along with it into the world beyond. A small world in itself—only a parish—but then my calling links it with infinity."

"I see; it is from the sources of love that you draw the supplies for happiness."

"Surely; without love one may be good, but one could scarcely be happy. No one can dream of a heaven except as the abode of love. What writer is it who says, 'How well the human heart was understood by him who first called God by the name of Father'?"

"I do not remember, but it is beautifully said. You evidently do not subscribe to the arguments in Decimus Roach's 'Approach to the Angels.'"

"Ah, Mr. Chillingly! your words teach me how lacerated a man's happiness may be if he does not keep the claws of vanity closely pared. I actually feel a keen pang when you speak to me of that eloquent panegyric on celibacy, ignorant that the only thing I ever published which I fancied was not without esteem by intellectual readers is a Reply to 'The Approach to the Angels'—a youthful book, written in the first year of my marriage. But it obtained success: I have just revised the tenth edition of it."

"That is the book I will select from your library. You will be pleased to hear that Mr. Roach, whom I saw at Oxford a few days ago, recants his opinions, and, at the age of fifty, is about to be married—he begs me to add, 'not for his own personal satisfaction.'"

"Going to be married!—Decimus Roach! I thought my Reply would convince him at last."

"I shall look to your Reply to remove some lingering doubts in my own mind."

"Doubts in favour of celibacy?"

"Well, if not for laymen, perhaps for a priesthood."

"The most forcible part of my Reply is on that head: read it attentively. I think that, of all sections of mankind, the clergy are those to whom, not only for their own sakes, but for the sake of the community, marriage should be most commended. Why, sir," continued the vicar, warming up into oratorical enthusiasm, "are you not aware that there are no homes in England from which men who have served and adorned their country have issued forth in such prodigal numbers as those of the clergy of our Church? What other class can produce a list so crowded with eminent names as we can boast in the sons we have reared and sent forth into the world? How many statesmen, soldiers, sailors, lawyers, physicians, authors, men of science, have been the sons of us village pastors? Naturally—for with us they receive careful education; they acquire of necessity the simple tastes and disciplined habits which lead to industry and perseverance; and, for the most part, they carry with them throughout life a purer moral code, a more systematic reverence for things and thoughts religious associated with their earliest images of affection and respect, than can be expected from the sons of laymen, whose parents are wholly temporal and worldly. Sir, I maintain that this is a cogent argument, to be considered well by the nation, not only in favour of a married clergy—for, on that score, a million of Roaches could not convert public opinion in this country—but in favour of the Church, the Established Church, which has been so fertile a nursery of illustrious laymen;

and I have often thought that one main and undetected cause of the lower tone of morality, public and private, of the greater corruption of manners, of the more prevalent scorn of religion which we see, for instance, in a country so civilised as France, is, that its clergy can train no sons to carry into the contests of earth the steadfast belief in accountability to Heaven."

"I thank you with a full heart," said Kenelm. "I shall ponder well over all that you have so earnestly said. I am already disposed to give up all lingering crotchets as to a bachelor clergy; but, as a layman, I fear that I shall never attain to the purified philanthropy of Mr. Decimus Roach, and if ever I do marry, it will be very much for my personal satisfaction."

Mr. Emlyn laughed good-humouredly, and, as they had now reached the bridge, shook hands with Kenelm, and walked homewards, along the brookside and through the burial-ground, with the alert step and the uplifted head of a man who has joy in life and admits of no fear in death.

CHAPTER XIV.

For the next two weeks or so Kenelm and Lily met, not indeed so often as the reader might suppose, but still frequently; five times at Mrs. Braefield's, once again at the Vicarage, and twice when Kenelm had called at Grasmere; and, being invited to stay to tea at one of those visits, he stayed the whole evening. Kenelm was more and more fascinated in proportion as he saw more and more of a creature so exquisitely strange to his experience. She was to him not only a poem, but a poem in the Sibylline Books—enigmatical, perplexing conjecture, and somehow or other mysteriously blending its interest with visions of the future.

Lily was indeed an enchanting combination of opposites rarely blended into harmony. Her ignorance of much that girls know before they number half her years, was so relieved by candid, innocent simplicity; so adorned by pretty fancies and sweet beliefs; and so contrasted and lit up by gleams of a knowledge that the young ladies we call well educated seldom exhibit—knowledge derived from quick observation of external nature, and impressionable susceptibility to its varying and subtle beauties. This knowledge had been perhaps first instilled, and subsequently nourished, by such poetry as she had not only learned by heart, but taken up as inseparable from the healthful circulation of her thoughts; not the poetry of our own day—most young ladies know enough of that—but selected fragments from the verse of old, most of them from poets now little read by the young of either sex, poets dear to spirits like Coleridge or Charles Lamb. None of them, however, so dear to her as the solemn melodies of Milton. Much of such poetry she had never read in books; it had been taught her in childhood by her guardian, the painter. And with all this imperfect, desultory culture, there was such dainty refinement in her every look and gesture, and such deep woman-tenderness of heart. Since Kenelm had commended

'Numa Pompilius' to her study, she had taken very lovingly to that old-fashioned romance, and was fond of talking to him about Egeria as of a creature who had really existed.

But what was the effect that he—the first man of years correspondent to her own with whom she had ever familiarly conversed—what was the effect that Kenelm Chillingly produced on the mind and the heart of Lily?

This was, after all, the question that puzzled him the most—not without reason: it might have puzzled the shrewdest bystander. The artless candour with which she manifested her liking to him was at variance with the ordinary character of maiden love; it seemed more the fondness of a child for a favourite brother. And it was this uncertainty that, in his own thoughts, justified Kenelm for lingering on, and believing that it was necessary to win, or at least to learn more of, her secret heart before he could venture to disclose his own. He did not flatter himself with the pleasing fear that he might be endangering her happiness; it was only his own that was risked. Then, in all those meetings, all those conversations to themselves, there had passed none of the words which commit our destiny to the will of another. If in the man's eyes love would force its way, Lily's frank, innocent gaze chilled it back again to its inward cell. Joyously as she would spring forward to meet him, there was no tell-tale blush on her cheek, no self-betraying tremor in her clear, sweet-toned voice. No; there had not yet been a moment when he could say to himself, "She loves me." Often he said to himself, "She knows not yet what love is."

In the intervals of time not passed in Lily's society, Kenelm would take long rambles with Mr. Emlyn, or saunter into Mrs. Braefield's drawing-room. For the former he conceived a more cordial sentiment of friendship than he entertained for any man of his own age—a friendship that admitted the noble elements of admiration and respect.

Charles Emlyn was one of those characters in which the colours appear pale unless the light be brought very close to them, and then each tint seems to change into a warmer and richer one. The manner which, at first, you would call merely gentle, becomes unaffectedly genial; the mind you at first might term inert, though well-informed, you now acknowledge to be full of disciplined vigour. Emlyn was not, however, without his little amiable foibles; and it was, perhaps, these that made him lovable. He was a great believer in human goodness, and very easily imposed upon by cunning appeals to "his well-known benevolence." He was disposed to overrate the excellence of all that he once took to his heart. He thought he had the best wife in the world, the best children, the best servants, the best beehive, the best pony, and the best house-dog. His parish was the most virtuous, his church the most picturesque, his vicarage the prettiest, certainly, in the whole shire—perhaps, in the whole kingdom. Probably it was this philosophy of optimism which contributed to lift him into the serene realm of æsthetic joy.

He was not without his dislikes as well as

likings. Though a liberal Churchman towards Protestant dissenters, he cherished the *odium theologicum* for all that savoured of Popery. Perhaps there was another cause for this besides the purely theological one. Early in life a young sister of his had been, to use his phrase, "secretly entrapped" into conversion to the Roman Catholic faith, and had since entered a convent. His affections had been deeply wounded by this loss to the range of them. Mr. Emlyn had also his little infirmities of self-esteem, rather than of vanity. Though he had seen very little of any world beyond that of his parish, he piqued himself on his knowledge of human nature and of practical affairs in general. Certainly no man had read more about them, especially in the books of the ancient classics. Perhaps it was owing to this that he so little understood Lily—a character to which the ancient classics afforded no counterpart nor clue; and perhaps it was this also that made Lily think him "so terribly grown up." Thus, despite his mild good nature, she did not get on very well with him.

The society of this amiable scholar pleased Kenelm the more, because the scholar evidently had not the remotest idea that Kenelm's sojourn at Cromwell Lodge was influenced by the vicinity to Grasmere. Mr. Emlyn was sure that he knew human nature, and practical affairs in general, too well to suppose that the heir to a rich baronet could dream of taking for wife a girl without fortune or rank, the orphan ward of a low-born artist only just struggling into reputation; or, indeed, that a Cambridge prizeman, who had evidently read much on grave and dry subjects, and who had no less evidently seen a great deal of polished society, could find any other attraction in a very imperfectly educated girl, who tamed butterflies and knew no more than they did of fashionable life, than Mr. Emlyn himself felt in the presence of a pretty wayward innocent child—the companion and friend of his Clemmy.

Mrs. Braefield was more discerning; but she had a good deal of tact, and did not as yet scare Kenelm away from her house by letting him see hov much she had discerned. She would not eve. tell her husband, who, absent from the placı on most mornings, was too absorbed in the cares ɔf his own business to interest himself much in the affairs of others.

Now Elsie, being still of a romantic turn of mind, had taken it into her head that Lily Mordaunt, if not actually the princess to be found in poetic dramas whose rank was for awhile kept concealed, was yet one of the higher-born daughters of the ancient race whose name she bore, and in that respect no derogatory alliance for Kenelm Chillingly. A conclusion she had arrived at from no better evidence than the well-bred appearance and manners of the aunt, and the exquisite delicacy of the niece's form and features, with the undefinable air of distinction which accompanied even her most careless and sportive moments. But Mrs. Braefield also had the wit to discover that under the infantine ways and phantasies of this almost self-taught girl, there lay, as yet undeveloped, the elements of a beautiful womanhood. So that altogether, from the very day she first re-encountered Kenelm, Elsie's thought had been that Lily was the wife to suit him. Once conceiving that idea, her natural strength of will made her resolve on giving all facilities to carry it out silently and unobtrusively, and therefore skilfully.

"I am so glad to think," she said one day, when Kenelm had joined her walk through the pleasant shrubberies in her garden ground, "that you have made such friends with Mr. Emlyn. Though all hereabouts like him so much for his goodness, there are few who can appreciate his learning. To you it must be a surprise as well as pleasure to find, in this quiet humdrum place, a companion so clever and well-informed; it compensates for your disappointment in discovering that our brook yields such bad sport."

"Don't disparage the brook; it yields the pleasantest banks on which to lie down under old pollard oaks at noon, or over which to saunter at morn and eve. Where those charms are absent even a salmon could not please. Yes; I rejoice to have made friends with Mr. Emlyn. I have learned a great deal from him, and am often asking myself whether I shall ever make peace with my conscience by putting what I have learned into practice."

"May I ask what special branch of learning is that?"

"I scarcely know how to define it. Suppose we call it 'Worth-whileism.' Among the New Ideas which I was recommended to study as those that must govern my generation, the Not-worth-while Idea holds a very high rank; and being myself naturally of calm and equable constitution, that new idea made the basis of my philosophical system. But since I have become intimate with Charles Emlyn I think there is a great deal to be said in favour of Worth-whileism, old idea though it be. I see a man who, with very commonplace materials for interest or amusement at his command, continues to be always interested or generally amused; I ask myself why and how? And it seems to me as if the cause started from fixed beliefs which settle his relations with God and man, and that settlement he will not allow any speculations to disturb. Be those beliefs questionable or not by others, at least they are such as cannot displease a Deity, and cannot fail to be kindly and useful to fellow mortals. Then he plants these beliefs on the soil of a happy and genial home, which tends to confirm and strengthen and call them into daily practice; and when he goes forth from home, even to the farthest verge of the circle that surrounds it, he carries with him the home influences of kindliness and use. Possibly my line of life may be drawn to the verge of a wider circle than his; but so much the better for interest and amusement, if it can be drawn from the same centre; namely, fixed beliefs daily warmed into vital action in the sunshine of a congenial home."

Mrs. Braefield listened to this speech with pleased attention, and as it came to its close, the name of Lily trembled on her tongue, for she divined that when he spoke of home Lily was in his thoughts; but she checked the impulse, and replied by a generalised platitude.

"Certainly the first thing in life is to secure a happy and congenial home. It must be a terrible trial for the best of us if we marry without love."

"Terrible, indeed, if the one loves and the other does not."

"That can scarcely be your case, Mr. Chillingly, for I am sure you could not marry where you did not love; and do not think I flatter you when I say that a man far less gifted than you can scarcely fail to be loved by the woman he wooes and wins."

Kenelm, in this respect one of the modestest of human beings, shook his head doubtingly, and was about to reply in self-disparagement, when, lifting his eyes and looking round, he halted mute and still as if rooted to the spot. They had entered the trellised circle through the roses of which he had first caught sight of the young face that had haunted him ever since.

"Ah!" he said abruptly; "I cannot stay longer here, dreaming away the work-day hours in a fairy ring. I am going to town to-day by the next train."

"You are coming back?"

"Of course—this evening. I left no address at my lodgings in London. There must be a large accumulation of letters—some, no doubt, from my father and mother. I am only going for them. Good-bye. How kindly you have listened to me!"

"Shall we fix a day next week for seeing the remains of the old Roman villa? I will ask Mrs. Cameron and her niece to be of the party."

"Any day you please," said Kenelm joyfully.

END OF VOL. III.

www.ingramcontent.com/pod-product-compliance
Lightning Source LLC
Chambersburg PA
CBHW020511270326
41926CB00008B/832

* 9 7 8 3 7 4 2 8 6 8 6 9 5 *